GET TO THE HEART

Written to help you with both sides of the phrase:

Getting to the heart of your information,

what's really going to make a difference

and getting to the hearts of those you present to

so they'll help you make it

Backstories Studio
1400 Marsten Road
Studio M
Burlingame, CA 94010
www.backstories.tv

Ordering Information:
Quantity sales. Special discounts are available on quantity purchases by corporations, associations, and others. For details, contact the publisher at the address above.

First Edition
Printed in the United States of America

ISBN: 978-0997853407

I'D LIKE TO THANK

My fellow storytellers at Backstories Studios:
Danica, Leigh and Morgan, for keeping me honest.

My wife, for helping me see so much more than I can on my own.

My co-writers, for making me sound smart.

The people I quote and reference, for making me look cool,
at least by association.

The two heroes you'll meet in this book: Sophia Kanety
and my real-life accountant, Alan "Mac" Watters who is actually
far more cool than Max (we made him read lines we wrote, and
we're not half as as cool as either of them)

Our Backstories clients, for giving me the inside view
that made this book actionable.

Dave and Catherine for sharing their stories so generously

Christopher, Davis, Darrel, and all my fellow Cheskin alum,
for teaching this jackass ad guy all about real business.

You, for reading it. I hope it serves you well.

You can lead
a revolution

to help move your company forward

or if you just want
to grow your skill set
and feel better
at the end of the day,

that's cool too.

Either way, I want you to have tools from the world's most successful storytelling form

so you'll get heard.

About Ted Frank

▶ Play Ted's Bio movie
It's at www.gettotheheartbook.com/ted)

PHOTO BY JANAE SHIELDS

I know this usually goes at the end, but I thought you might like to know who you'll be spending all these pages with.

My road to movie-style storytelling was both lucky and wacky. First, advertising taught me to be simple. Then consumer insights taught me about people and why they do what they do. Working in strategy taught me about how big corporations really work, and what keeps them from working. My second stint in advertising led me to film classes, where I started really looking at how movies tell stories. All of these brought me to Backstories, the place where my colleagues and I take 100-page PowerPoint decks and turn them into three- to five-minute movies. But knowing that not everyone has the resources to make movies every day led me to create workshops, and subsequently to this book. I want you and your department to have a new set of tools to make your information easy to get, and easy to get behind. So everyone—project leads, execs, and companies—can make a bigger difference.

Notes that will make reading this book easier and more fulfilling

You can use all these principles in PowerPoint
I will talk a lot about movies, but don't focus on the medium. Focus on the *way* movies tell stories. All their principles can be applied to a PowerPoint presentation, and should be. It will make the conference room a much better place for everyone.

Stakeholders
I use the word "stakeholders" as a blanket term for anyone you present to. Colleagues, executives, your direct boss, strategic partners like ad agencies, investors, clients, and of course, prospective clients.

"Click to play" movies
You'l see photos throughout this book a triangular play button. They'rere actually movies. If you've got the interactive version of this book, you can just click on them. If you've got the printed version, there's a URL right after the words "click to play." I know it's a pain the butt if you have to go to the URL, but the movies bring the concepts to life. So you'll be glad you did.

www.gettotheheartbook.com website
I've set up a web site (actually, my lead editor, Danica, did) that has all the movies in this book, a series of Strategic Storytelling video blogs, an area where you can ask questions.

Get to the Heart Workshops
Our workshops turn the lessons in this book into experiences that are even more rich, interactive and fun. The biggest difference, though, is that instead of just using my examples, if your company signs up for a workshop, we'll use one of your actual presentations as the main example, so you can easily see how well the principles work. It's also BYOP (bring your own presentation) for everyone who attends, so by the end of the day, everyone comes away not only with mad skills, but an elevated presentation. You can find out more at www.gettotheheartbook.com.

Contents

CHAPTER 1

Why It's So (blanking) Hard To Get Heard

and is storytelling the answer?

I gave a presentation at a big food company. My team and I worked for two months on a research and strategy project for one of their cornerstone brands that had been bleeding market share for a long time. The stakes were huge—if they could reverse the trend, it would be worth millions to the company, so they'd spent $100,000 on the project. Now it was time to present to their top leadership.

Fun fact about goldfish
coming right up

When the executives walked in, I heard some of them talking about a movie they'd seen. They settled in and we took them through our PowerPoint presentation. I thought it went well. Our findings were insightful and actionable, our strategy to gain new customers was both opportunistic and right in the company's wheelhouse, and the presentation itself was smooth. But when we finished our last slide, the execs went right back to talking about the movie.

In the end, none of our recommendations were implemented. The brand is still technically alive, but I rarely see it in stores anymore. Their $100,000 might as well have gone in the garbage—or in the filing cabinet where our deck may still be collecting dust.

You're reading this book, so I imagine you've experienced a project like that. You probably had sophisticated recommendations and powerful data that could have made a huge difference. Your company might have even spent a ton on your project, like that food company did on mine. But for some reason, your team and your work still got ignored.

If that's true, I hope it will make you feel to better to know you're not alone. I've seen it happen to many really smart, dedicated people who worked their butts off and came back with gold for the clients. Then they heard...nothing.

The magnitude of the problem really hit me when I attended a workshop led by two guys from one of America's largest companies. The genesis of their workshop came to them while sitting in a presentation. Both started feeling serious déjà vu. Then they realized why. The year before, they had seen nearly the same presentation, but from a different team. They were the only ones who remembered it, though. Not even the group who led that day's presentation knew about the previous project. The two guys asked around their company and found similar stories of redundant projects. Other people attending the workshop said they had seen it at their companies as well.

So it's definitely not just you. Presentations going in one ear and out the other is happening everywhere.

But why?
Shrinking attention spans, perhaps? Actually, that is part of it. According to the Statistic Brain Research Institute (SBRI), from 2000 to 2015, the average attention span has dropped by 3.75 seconds, hovering somewhere around 8.25 seconds.

SBRI also cited this fun fact: you know who has a higher attention span than us? Your kid's goldfish. At nine seconds, a goldfish can pay attention for nearly a full second longer than we can. (But then, the report doesn't indicate whether they made the goldfish watch PowerPoint slides.)

So if our audiences can't be as attentive as goldfish, what can we do? Well, the first step is to look a little deeper at what our audiences deal with and why it's so hard for them to sustain attention.

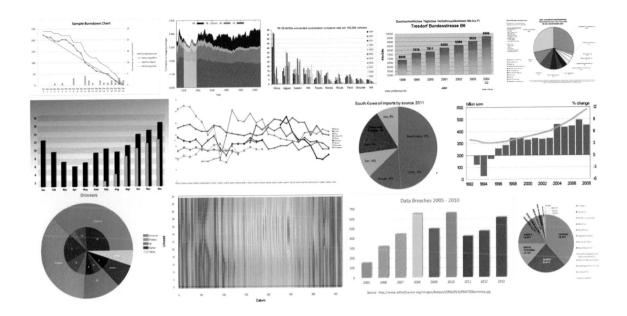

Spend a minute in their shoes

Your stakeholders are just as dedicated as you are. They sincerely want to hear you or they wouldn't give up their time to be at your meeting. But guess how many meetings they have to attend each day? The answer I usually hear is six to eight.

Can you imagine sitting through that many meetings every day? Each one in a dim conference room, each one showing the same thing: slides on a screen. Charts and bullet points, charts and bullet points—all day long—most read by a presenter sitting at the opposite end of the room from the screen, forcing them to either crane their necks back and forth, or do what any sane person in their shoes would do: listen to the faceless voice and stare at the bullets and charts as they do their thing. Over and over and over again.

If you were them, wouldn't all those words and slides start to blur? Wouldn't your mind drift to things you have to do, emails you need to write, where to pick up dinner? Mmmm...dinner.

I'm sure you've seen the eye-glazing trance that comes from this overexposure to charts and bullets. I call it the "Same What?"

Same

Until you really look at a chart or have it explained to you, they all look the same. Look at the set above from a Creative Commons search I just ran. See what I mean? Every now and then you get an area graph or a trend chart, but mostly, it's bars and pies, bars and pies. All of the charts also have similar colors, fonts, and layouts because they all come from similar Excel or PowerPoint templates. There's no beacon for your stakeholders' eyes to gravitate toward.

Bullet points have a little more differentiation. But when formatted to the corporate template, they'll also look similar until you read them. So, again, no immediate signal for the eye to tell the brain, "Wake up. This is new."

What?

Then there's the fact that our eyes see a chart as just a bunch of colored shapes and lines. Meaning has to be brought into it, by either the small pieces of text or the narration of the person presenting it. Either way, it requires work on the part of the audience to make that leap from these abstract shapes to full understanding. And when you see hundreds of charts a day, like most stakeholders do, that work adds up—to a degree no goldfish ever has to face.

Bullets should be easier for stakeholders because they can read them. Unfortunately, most presenters also read their bullets out loud, but cannot speak as fast as their stakeholders can read them onscreen, so eyes and ears get completely out of sync and then brains have to do all kinds of work to sort it out.

It's no wonder so much key information gets lost. Actually, let's take a second and feel it for ourselves. Go ask someone to read this paragraph to you aloud while you try to read it silently. Did it mess you up? Did you find the person's voice annoying? That's what happens in so many presentations.

I came across a great book by Christopher Frank (no relation) and Paul Magnone. They interviewed tons of executives about their experiences in meetings and how hard it is to take in information. Their title summed it up perfectly: *Drinking from the Fire Hose*. Because that's how the execs said they felt. Even though they're thirsty for information, they're getting hit by so much, so fast, they can't actually take most of it in.

I heard the same from execs I interviewed. Here's two:

> Andy Cunningham, the Silicon Valley legend who heads up Cunningham Collective and was the PR lead for the Apple Macintosh, told me: "When I get too much information, I just shut down."

Andy's incredibly curious and an amazing listener. I can tell you that she does not like to shut down. It's just inevitable when you're facing the firehose.

> Michael Perman, the Dean of Innovation at Gap, Inc., is another exec who's naturally curious. It feeds his creative spark. But he too sits in a lot of meetings. He told me: "Too much information is just a blur."

This overwhelm is what made execs shout out "Get it down to 5 slides!" a few years ago, only to find out that people just shrunk the text so they could cram in more. But it's also why today execs keep asking for something different. With more and more data hitting them every day, they can't keep up with all the "same whats" that appear in slide after slide after slide. Execs

Paul Magnone and Christopher Frank researched execs and their experiences with information. Their conclusion: it feels like trying to drink from a firehose. So much information is hitting them, and yet they can't take it all in.

need something they can grab onto, which is why so many of them are asking for stories.

So is story the answer?

Story may not be the only answer, but I'm going with the execs on this one, because I know stories can help you slow down the firehose, get the execs the info they need, and get your project the buy-in it deserves.

After all, stories have always been how we understand the world and abstract concepts. We explain things to one another every day through stories and use them to prove our points, like when you tell your friends about the idiots and maniacs on the road. You always include a story about what happened to you so they'll understand and agree. Without stories, facts would flutter in the wind. They, and the examples told within them, help us grab ahold of the facts, relate to them, and in some cases, change our beliefs. They're completely natural to us as a way to communicate, bond, and entertain ourselves.

And yet, in business presentations and reports, this natural communication tool gets left behind. Perhaps

our desire to look smart and scientific led us to fixate on charts. Perhaps our desire to be pithy led us to lean on bullet points. More likely, it's because when we first open up PowerPoint, that's how the templates are already set up: bullets and charts.

To be fair, both of those tools can be highly effective. Bullets can indeed help us be more concise and make certain information stand out. Charts can show us the relationship between data points like no one's business, and infographics can make them easier, cooler, and more fun. Headlines can sum it up for us, and metaphors can put things into a tasty nutshell. But when you want your stakeholders to truly "get it," believe you on a deeper level, and care enough about what you're saying to actually get off their butts and do something, none of those tools are nearly as powerful as a well-told story.

Stories will take you further

Stories give you all that because they provide the context that makes information meaningful. In Chapter 3, we'll tell you a lot more, but for now, here's the gist: when you frame your information as a story—with char-

"I've seen it in so many contexts—in my business life in particular—where stories are convincing. Where the thing that triggers the Aha! moment is what convinces you to do something."

- David Hornik, August Capital

acters, settings, and action—you transform it from an abstract, unmanageable firehose into an experience that's easier and more concrete for people to remember. What's more, when your story evokes emotion, people won't just listen or watch; they'll <u>care</u>, and most importantly, care enough to make things happen.

Speaking of making things happen, venture capitalist David Hornik of August Capital has backed a lot of highly successful startups. Unfortunately, he also has to sit through a lot of meetings, so he's felt the blast of countless firehoses. But he's also felt the power of story, and told us:

> "I've seen it in so many contexts—in my business life in particular—where stories are convincing. Where the thing that triggers the Aha! moment is what convinces you to do something."

Michael Perman and his colleagues at Gap, Inc. have a tough job. They have to keep the idea machine flowing at a company that reinvents its product line every three months. To make that happen, they have to inspire thousands of people, so Michael often turns to stories, because, as he puts it:

> "Stories within a corporate environment provide meaning. They take people to a place that they can't get to themselves."

Now let's look at the science
To be honest, I am inherently lazy, so kudos to the TED conference for having a convenient search bar on their web site that pointed me to two scientists firmly enmeshed in the study of story. I encourage you to visit www.ted.com and watch their presentations, and don't forget to Google these great minds and see even more of their work.

Dr. Paul Zak heads the Center for Neuroeconomic Studies at Claremont Graduate University. We'll hear from Dr. Zak throughout this book, be-

"Stories within a corporate environment provide meaning. They take people to a place that they can't get to themselves."

- Michael Perman
Dean of Innovation
Gap, Inc.

cause we got to interview him and see him in action. Super nice guy, too.

Dr. Zak and his colleagues have conducted many experiments on the way our brains and bodies react to the delivery of information. In particular, they study oxytocin, this amazing chemical our brains produce that, like dopamine or endorphins, makes us feel really good. It also makes us more open, thoughtful, loving, generous, and inspired—emotions that are good to have on your side when trying to convince stakeholders to take a chance on an initiative you know will do a lot of good. Hugs and positive human interaction spike oxytocin. We've all felt that. But guess what? So does a story. Here's Dr. Zak:

> "When we watch a story, our brains release oxytocin. And what happens? It relaxes us, makes us more empathic, more connected to the people around us...
>
> "Effective stories change people's behaviors. We've shown that in laboratories and field studies we can, through storytelling, induce people to engage in costly behaviors—donating money to charity, for example."

I'm sure you've felt that, too. Save The Children did a fundraising experiment: half of their leaflets showed big stats like millions of kids in poverty; the other half featured a story about one little girl. The story brought in more than twice as much money.

So stories can definitely persuade us in the moment, but Dr. Zak and his colleagues also wanted to see if stories stuck with people longer than other forms of information:

> "Data is super important. I'm a data guy, no question about it, but from an impact perspective, human-scale stories that also embody emotion have much more impact, both in the moment and later on down the road."

So that's people on an individual level. Now let's talk about the power of story to unite a group. And for that, let me introduce you to another TED fellow, Princeton professor Dr. Uri Hasson.

In his lab, Dr. Hasson used functional magnetic resonance imaging (fMRI) to see what happens when five people listen to the same story told aloud. Before the recording began, their brains showed rather different activity. But then, once they began to hear the story, their brain activity aligned. Story brought them together, not only figuratively, but neurologically. It's that unifying and powerful.

So they upped the ante and tried the experiment with one story told in different languages. They got the same result. Even when the words differed, people's brains still aligned.

That's amazingly powerful stuff when you think about a multinational company like Gap. With stores all over the

"In terms of impact, this blows the standard PowerPoint presentation to bits."

– Dr. Paul Zak, Harvard Business Review

world, it has to be insanely challenging to align people around a new product, policy, or vision. With story, they have a powerful way to do it.

And for those of us who don't have global workforces, but are focused on one presentation in one conference room with a handful of stakeholders, let me quote Dr. Zak once more, this time from *Harvard Business Review*:

> "My experiments show that character-driven stories with emotional content result in a better understanding of the key points a speaker wants to make and better recall of these points weeks later. In terms of making impact, this blows the standard PowerPoint presentation to bits."

And the timing for story couldn't be better

While execs are clamoring, people have not been answering. Frankly, the bar has never been lower. So if you can strike now and bring your stakeholders a story, you'll make a huge and meaningful difference for your company—far more than some showboating loudmouth trying to "disrupt" everything.

But are all stories equal?

I think not. I've been in corporate America a long, long time and I've seen countless examples of storytelling. I've seen data visualization, improv, and dozens of "meet ___" slides. I've seen some presenters excel with these methods, but I've seen many others get mired in more muck than they began with.

Some of these methods just ask too much of us. For example, I've seen metaphors work perfectly at the beginning of a presentation, but then after a while, feel really forced. I've seen presenters try to explain diagrams so complicated that they got lost in their own explanation. And I've seen people not even get that far because they knew that even if they could visualize their data, they couldn't draw their visualization.

TWO TYPES OF STORIES WHERE PEOPLE TEND TO STRUGGLE

Metaphor-based visualizations can be amazing, but carrying the metaphor through more than one slide and drawing all the visuals well can be difficult.

A "meet __" slide, clearly a stock photo. They're easy to carry out, but stakeholders can't truly relate to them if they don't feel real or give enough story.

Other methods might be easier, but can lack the structure you really need to tell a story well. I've seen stock photos that not only looked fake, but it was obvious the presenters were embarrassed to show them.

With all these methods, I've watched the confidence and credibility of presenters crumble. I really felt for them because I know they were giving it their best, but they just didn't have a method that fit their information, objectives, or the situations that are unique to corporate environments.

So I decided to find or develop a storytelling method that <u>would</u> work for real corporate presentations. One that could give your stakeholders what they were clamoring for, and beyond. One that does what the scientists say it will do: align their brains to be more open to your ideas.

But I also wanted it to be easy for you to learn and become your natural tool, to take you from everyday data to those high-stakes quarterly presentations, when you really need to hit it out of the park.

And I wanted it to be something you could carry out with aplomb. That wouldn't weigh you down or crush your confidence, but would spike it along with your oxytocin. Because when you and your team work as hard as you do, you deserve a method that will not only get your information heard, but make you look and feel like an expert.

I found that story method in a place everyone already appreciates and loves: the movies.

Why movies?

Remember those execs at the big food company from the beginning of this chapter? Both before and after my presentation, they were all talking about a movie. It clearly made more of an impression on them than we did with our PowerPoint slides.

So that made me wonder: how are movies successful at making us love them—a love so strong that we hang movie posters on our walls and wear their T-shirts? What makes them so memorable that you can overhear someone saying a line from a movie and instantly recognize it?

In fact, let's put it to the test right now. Below are five lines from movies. How many of them do you recognize?

"There's no place like home."

"Go ahead. Make my day."

"Toga! Toga! Toga!"

"I'll make him an offer he can't refuse."

"Use the Force, Luke!"

I'll bet you can identify most of those lines—and they're all from movies at least thirty-five years old. The quote people recognize most is from a film released in 1939.

Can you imagine your projects having that kind of resonance? Can you imagine your colleagues as they leave your presentation, quoting your words and evangelizing your ideas as they walk into another meeting, like my movie-loving clients back at the mega-food company?

It's not just the camera that makes movies the most successful story format in the world today.

It's also the <u>way</u> movies tell stories, the approaches they take.

The slide-sorter view in PowerPoint is not unlike a movie storyboard, so later in this book, we'll learn how to treat our slides in the same ways screenwriters and directors treat their scenes.

Yeah, but doesn't that mean you need video?

Nope. There are definitely times when video is highly advantageous, and we'll cover those when we get to Section 2 and high-stakes presentations. But I know that PowerPoint decks are your bread and butter, so first and foremost, I want to find movie strategies you could bring to your deck.

It's not actually that hard—it's not just the camera that makes movies the most successful story format in the world today. It's also the *way* movies tell their stories, the approaches they take. Like being quick, visual, and emotionally affecting. Those are traits every stakeholder in every corporation wants to see more of, and no one does them better than movies and TV. (I include both in a blanket term I call "movie-style storytelling" because they follow similar approaches.) So step by step, we'll be mapping the strategies of the screenwriters, directors and editors, and applying them to the kinds of decks and presentations you do, including the objectives, requirements, tools, and political nonsense that make up your actual work day.

Here are a few examples:

Movies cut to the chase

Watch your favorite movies or TV shows and you'll see how concise they are. That economy is baked into movies and TV from the start because fewer scenes and shots means less time and budget. So screenwriters are trained to cut scenes that are not absolutely necessary. For example, when a movie character is going to work, it's explained in just a few shots: grab the bag, walk out the door, drive the car, walk into the office.

Because what moviemakers discovered is that we don't need the stuff in between. We not only don't miss it, but we actually remember more of the story because the important scenes aren't bogged down by unimportant ones.

The same is true for presentation decks, so I'll help you cut out the unimportant slides that get in the way of your key points. The results will be the same. You'll be pithy, relevant, swift, and substantial. And your stakeholders will remember more.

Movies make that chase real

Because movies are a visual and sensory story format, they can make stories even more real for us, with far less effort from our brains. They show it to us on screen, so we can see it, hear it, and know exactly what we're dealing with. Not only that, we see and hear it in the same way as the people next to us. This is incredibly important when you think about the number of folks who will need to take your information and run with it. With words or charts or bullets, there are often multiple ways your information can be interpreted, but with a visual, people align and are able to absorb and share your information correctly.

For instance, if I give you the word "fish," do you think of a fish swimming in the ocean or a piece of fish on a plate? Now take a look at the fish on the right. See what I mean? No doubt what that is. So we'll cover how to show your story visually and minimize the kinds of deviations that come with just the word "fish." You won't always have an audio component like movies do, but you'll still be able to create the same lightning-fast shared understanding.

You'll also be focusing on visualizing real situations, not just metaphor. This makes it simpler for your stakeholders to understand because they'll be seeing real life, and it also makes it easier to find your visual. You can still draw it or have it drawn, but you can just as easily find a photo or take one yourself because we'll be drawing from real life.

Movies make you scared and excited to be in the chase

Those educational films we saw in school (not to mention corporate videos) may stop at being simple and real, but mov-

Now that we can all see it, is there any doubt what kind of fish I'm talking about?

HERE'S WHAT IN STORE FOR YOU

		MAKE IT SIMPLE	MAKE IT REAL		MAKE IT STICK
GROUND WE'LL COVER	**1** SECTION	Make your presentations: *More concise* *More relevant* *More focused*	Make your presentations: *More visual* *More relatable* *More memorable* *Tell a cohesive story*	**2** SECTION	Make your presentations: *Fit their natural learning style* *Consider their aspirations and fears*
RESULT YOU'LL SEE		And stakeholders will: *Find it easier* *Appreciate your pith*	And stakeholders will: *Really get it* *Tell others*		And stakeholders will: *Really listen* *Be able to work with it*

ies take it one step further by making you *feel* what the characters feel. They make it emotional. And that's what gives movies so much power. They make us forget about our own world and go into the hero's experience, leading us into their cause. They have to get the girl or the prize or true justice, so we have to see them get it.

It's a power that few other forms of communication possess. So in the second half of the book, we'll harness some of that emotional power. You'll learn how to evoke emotion in your stakeholders so they'll feel the need you want them to feel and inspire them to join your cause.

Your storytelling will go much deeper

Above, on the top row, you'll see a list of the various topics I'll cover throughout this book. On the bottom row, you'll see how these techniques will help you connect with your stakeholders. Yep, I aim to help you create stories that will take you much further and deeper, so you can make a bigger difference.

But we'll start at the beginning

This book is divided into two parts. We'll start with your everyday work—your charts, bullets, typical presentation and report decks—and transform them into something about halfway between a storyboard and a TED

OPEN STRONG	SHOW HEROES IN ACTION	EVOKE THE CAUSE

Make your presentations:
  Take command of the room
  Establish urgency
  Establish credibility
	Make your presentations:
	  Provide a clear picture of who,
	    what, where, and why
	  Emotionally gripping and personal
		Make your presentations:
		  A clear opportunity they can seize
		  A way to win
		  A rallying call to make a difference

And stakeholders will:
  Forget about their phones and
    really listen
  Feel you are too important
    to ignore
	And stakeholders will:
	  Feel the need
	  See the opportunities
	  Want to help
		And stakeholders will:
		  Know what they need to do
		  Have a desire to do it
		  Feel confident enough to lead others

presentation. And just like TED speakers, your ability to be concise, clear, and visual will make your stakeholders appreciate and value you more. They'll also relay your information more accurately and come to you earlier and more often, with questions that are more strategic. You'll elevate your stature and satisfaction and make contributions on a higher level.

Which means you'll be excited for Section 2 of the book, because that's where we'll cover the higher-level presentations you'll be doing a lot more of. In that section, you'll learn to hit stakeholders at a much deeper level, going beyond just delivering understanding to actually engag-ing their emotions and releasing their oxytocin, so they come in open and focused, and come away inspired and confident about green lighting your initiative.

To get there, our movie-meets-corporate reality ap-proach will follow a map that shows you when and how to do things like create urgency and credibility, and how to build a rallying cause for your initiative. I won't lie—it may be more work than you're used to, but the feel-ing you'll get from having that much command over the room, and the response you'll see and feel from your stakeholders will be so gratifying, I guarantee you won't want to go back.

1 | TRANSFORMING YOUR EVERY DAY

Say goodbye to endless charts and bullets
and all the boredom that comes with them.

Say hello to visual stories that everyone
will get. And get behind.

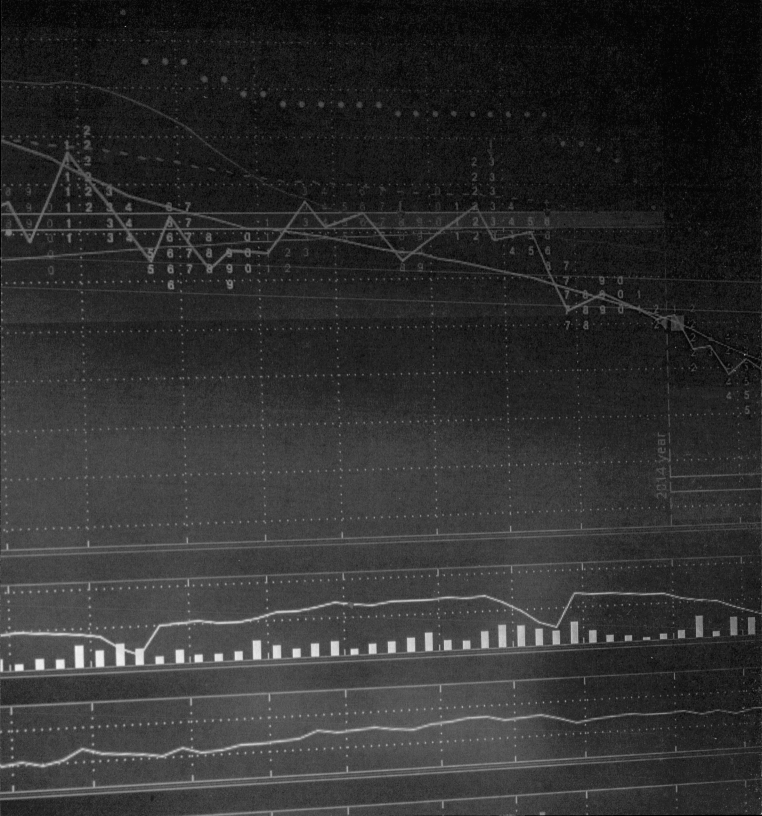

CHAPTER 2

Make It Simple

so everyone can get on board

Everyone, especially in a conference room, wants presentations to be simple. Unfortunately, this is not an easy feat for the people who prepare those presentations. Especially when they've been working on a project for a long time, and even more so when they're smart and can hold all that information in their heads—all those factors conspire to drive them deeper into the weeds.

We've all been there, on both the giving and receiving end. When I try to listen to someone in the weeds, it often feels like the visual to the right. I'm listening, I'm concentrating, and I really want the presentation to go somewhere, but I just keep feeling more confused.

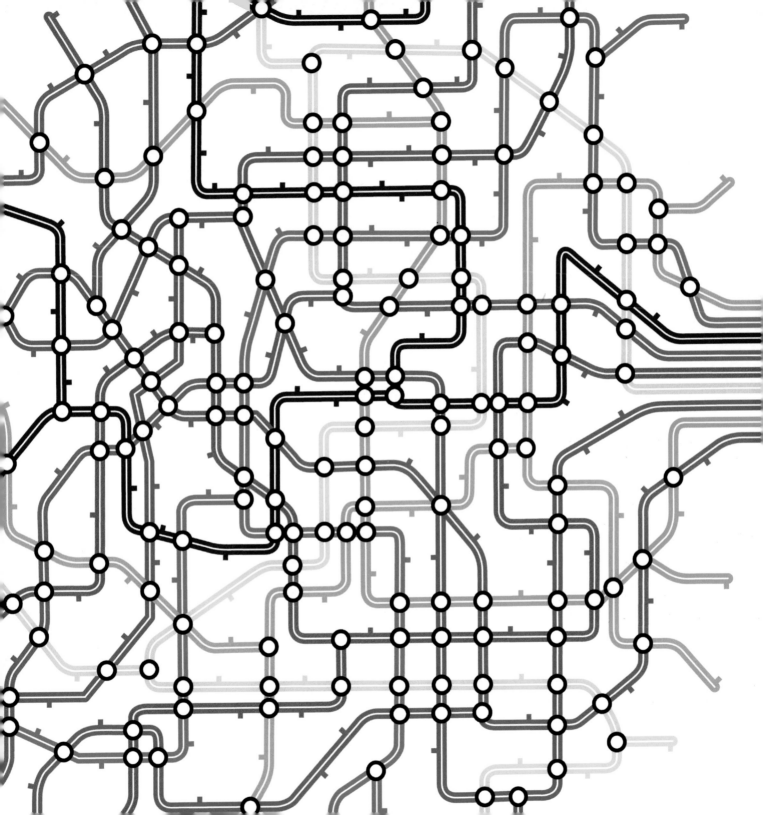

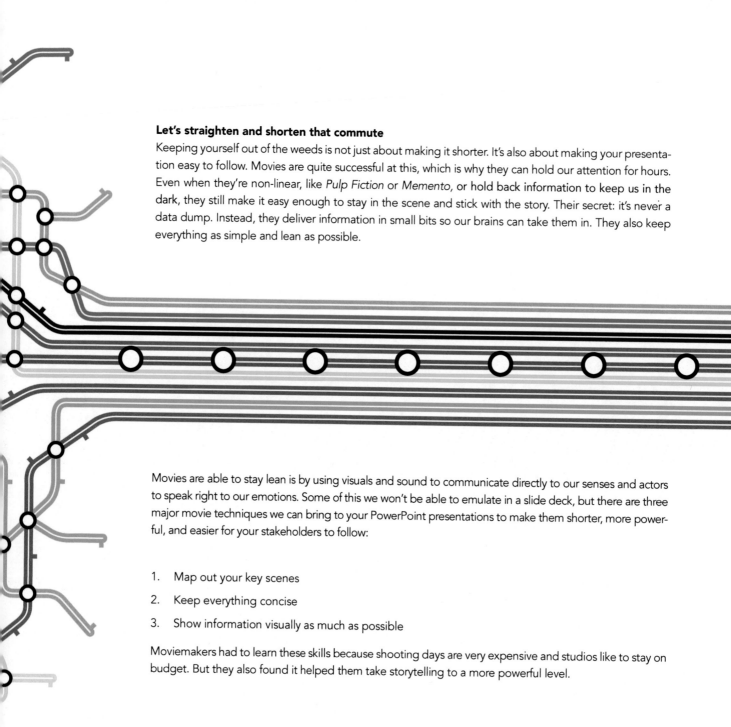

Let's straighten and shorten that commute

Keeping yourself out of the weeds is not just about making it shorter. It's also about making your presentation easy to follow. Movies are quite successful at this, which is why they can hold our attention for hours. Even when they're non-linear, like *Pulp Fiction* or *Memento,* or hold back information to keep us in the dark, they still make it easy enough to stay in the scene and stick with the story. Their secret: it's never a data dump. Instead, they deliver information in small bits so our brains can take them in. They also keep everything as simple and lean as possible.

Movies are able to stay lean is by using visuals and sound to communicate directly to our senses and actors to speak right to our emotions. Some of this we won't be able to emulate in a slide deck, but there are three major movie techniques we can bring to your PowerPoint presentations to make them shorter, more powerful, and easier for your stakeholders to follow:

1. Map out your key scenes

2. Keep everything concise

3. Show information visually as much as possible

Moviemakers had to learn these skills because shooting days are very expensive and studios like to stay on budget. But they also found it helped them take storytelling to a more powerful level.

Identifying key scenes

How many key scenes would you imagine a typical movie has? Ten? Twenty? In most movies, it's actually just three. There's the scene that kicks the story into motion, the turning point, and the climax. So the first thing screenwriters do is map out those key scenes.

Coming up with just three ideas makes it far more manageable, and it also makes the rest of the process easier—with those key scenes as markers, screenwriters know exactly where they need to go. And all of the other scenes are then given a specific job: drive the story toward the next key scene (or the closing credits).

A ton of work still goes into fleshing everything out and fine-tuning the script, but the screenwriter's energy always has direction so they don't feel lost like so many of us do. It's also how some movies are written in a week. Sylvester Stallone actually wrote *Rocky* in less than four days, and we all know that success story.

Your three key scenes

You can apply this same three-scene approach to your deck. Sticking with the movie convention of three may sound arbitrary because your strategic story has completely different objectives than a movie, but it's actually a good rule. The truth is that most people can only remember three or four points from a presentation, so if you put more emphasis on those, you get to decide what your stakeholders remember.

To figure out your three key points and to get your story rolling on a pithy, relevant path, start with the one question that surprisingly few people ask before starting a presentation:

How many key scenes would you imagine a typical movie would have? Ten? Twenty?

Not even close.

Question #1:
What do your stakeholders need to do?

Do they need to refine a product feature? Reposition a brand? Get buy-in from a key customer? What do *they* need to do overall?

Going beyond your own project objectives to theirs will immediately focus your deck on the information that will make the biggest difference to your stakeholders. It positions you as a big-picture thinker who can see the real issues.

Question #2:
What are the three most important things they need to know to do it right?

Now that you know what they need to do, take a look through your information and ask yourself: what are the three most important things they need to know to do it right?

Feel free to write a long list first, then cull it down, or group a series of topics into larger buckets if that's easier. But cap it at the three points you'll emphasize so you can help your stakeholders see what's most important.

Take them on a moving journey

Now it's time to plot out those points to form the backbone of your story. This should be done by feel as much as by thought. Yes, their order absolutely needs to be logical and if one point has to be understood before you can understand the other two, then it needs to go first. Similarly, if your three key points are chronological or sequential, go with the way they would naturally flow.

But if the order isn't already dictated, think about your stakeholders for another minute. What order would provoke—then keep heightening—their intrigue or feeling of opportunity? Maybe you start with the least interesting, most obvious point, then expand out to the most compelling eye-opener. That way, it will draw everyone in and create its own energy.

It's kind of like going to a fancy dinner; they never start with the main course. First, they build your desire with smaller items like appetizers and salad—tasty, but never fully satisfying. Because then comes the big course you've been waiting for, and then, just when you think you're satisfied, dessert!

It's just more magical that way.

The scenes in between

Earlier I wrote that once a screenwriter maps out the three key scenes, the job of the other scenes was to "drive" the story toward the next key scene. This is a subtle but key difference that keeps us engaged and on the edge of our seats. They don't make the point then substantiate it like a high school essay (or most presentations) because they know you'll lose interest. It would be like telling the punch line before the joke. Instead, they flip it and put the supporting information first, but they also do it in a way that drives you toward their key

The Big **Questions:**

What do your stakeholders need to do?

What are the three most important things they need to know to do it right?

These will help you turn down the firehose and give your stakeholders something they can actually drink.

point. For instance, in *Jaws*, you see the swimmer from above water, then below the water so we know she's vulnerable, then we see the fin, and then...the attack. They don't start with the attack because they know we'll lose interest. Then, once the attack is over, they move on to driving toward the next big point.

You can do the same thing in your presentations—keep interest their heightened. Keep reading and you'll soon see a perfect example.

Live and let die

Even with their brevity, completed scripts and the first edit of a movie can still be too long and thick, thick, thick with weeds. So Hollywood has another technique they call "killing your babies." (I apologize to all parents and people with a heart. It's their expression, not mine). They call it that because it's the incredibly painful exercise of cutting out the stuff you think is great or important (your "babies"), but to everyone else, is mucking up your story.

You can get to a leaner, more powerful story by "killing your babies," as they say in Hollywood.

This homicide is almost always committed by someone with a fresh perspective. The director comes in and kills the screenwriters' babies, then the editor kills the directors' babies. And everyone allows it because they know it makes the story leaner, stronger, and easier to follow.

Ira Glass, host of the popular radio show *This American Life*, once said: "By killing, you make something else even better live." He also said that what makes things really good are ruthless people willing to rework what they've made.

Now let's look at you and your presentation. If you've got weeds or a firehose going—chances are, you've got one big nursery full of your babies, usually information you've worked so hard to find and develop, you can't see that it's not nearly as important as your key points. So like filmmakers, we owe it to ourselves and our colleagues to see them for what they truly are: evil babies holding you back from making a real impact.

So just like the screenwriter needs the director and the director needs the editor, go find some buddies at your company who don't work on your projects—that is crucial—so they can give you the perspective of someone seeing your information for the first time.

Tell your new elite baby-killing squad the answers to the Big2 questions (what do your stakeholders need to do and what information will enable them to do it right), then give them your presentation deck. Ask them to separate the points and slides that help you get there from those that don't. Insist that they be ruthless. And even though it will hurt like hell, listen to them and throw out the superfluous slides. Kill your babies, further your story, and get your key points heard.

How I learned to kill my babies

This story didn't actually happen to me. My story is actually quite convoluted, so I'm going make my point in a more powerful way by co-opting one I heard from an old colleague. I feel okay doing it—I've lived this type of experience so many times, it feels like my story. And it's the perfect tale to show you the payoff of killing your babies…

I started my career as a creative at an ad agency. The first ad I had to write was for a gym chain called Holiday Health Spa. (Today it's part of 24-Hour Fitness and L.A. Fitness.) Back in 1990, when this story takes place, the spokesperson for Holiday Health Spa was the Eagles' Glenn Frey. The Eagles were still a popular band, but they were about ten years past their heyday.

The art for the ad was to be two photos: Glenn back in his rock-star days, long-haired and wild; contrasted with a new shot of Glenn, all buffed out and posing with a barbell at Holiday Health Spa.

My job was to write the ad, so the first thing I did was call Glenn on the phone. Awesome guy and super hilarious. And Glenn starts telling me his story: how when he was with the Eagles, he got to travel the world, play cool music with his best friends, party every night, and meet tons of chicks.

"If you say too much, you end up saying nothing."

Then, if you've ever seen VH1's *Behind the Music*, you know the next part: the partying takes over, the hits stop coming, the band breaks up, the chicks go away.

But Glenn is a little wiser than your average rock star, so he starts lifting weights and getting in shape. Pretty soon he's looking better, feeling better, and lo and behold, the chicks come back—all thanks to Holiday Health Spa.

So I write up the ad, walk it over to my creative director, and stand smugly, waiting for my promotion. But my creative director doesn't even read it. He hands it right back and says, "Cut it."

"How much?" I ask. His harsh response: "A lot."

"But it's awesome," I plead.

"I'm sure it is," he says, "but no one's going to read it."

Then he says something to me I will never forget: "If you say too much, you end up saying nothing."

If you say too much, you end up saying nothing. Makes so much sense now, but back then I was an immature idiot, so I just sigh, to which he replies, "You don't believe me? Take it down to the admins and show them. Give them five minutes with your ad and ask them, 'What did you get out of it?' Don't ask them if they like it. Ask them what they *got* out of it."

So I do. I head downstairs to the admins and hand my ad to the first one. Immediately, though, I get it shoved right back in my face, along with an expression I'd rather forget.

Creative director 1, Ted 0.

I go to the next admin. She agrees to read it, so I come back five minutes later. "What did you get out of the ad?" I ask.

She says, "Oh, it's great. Good work."

I ask again. "But what did you get out of the ad?"

The original draft (photo shoot would come later)

The simplified ad

She doesn't say anything, so I ask, "Did you read it?"

She shrugs her shoulders. "I started to."

Tail between my legs, I go back upstairs and cut the ad. I cut so much that it feels like I sucked the soul out of it. Then I hand my creative director the shortened, soul-sucked version, hoping he's going to relieve my pain. But just as quickly as last time, he shakes his head and says, "It's still too long."

Then he points to the text and crosses it out. All of it.

I start to freak out, so he turns to me and says, "When you think about what this ad needs to do, what people need to get from it, what is it really about?"

I take a second to think, and then say, "It's about turning your life around."

"Exactly," he says, pointing to the page. "And there are four words that hit that perfectly. Right here," he says as he circles "Hard Rock" and "Rock Hard" in my headline. "Put 'em right under the photos and you got your ad. Now mock it up and take it to the admins."

So I do, and...have you ever been punched in the gut? I hand it to the admin and she doesn't need five minutes. She doesn't even need five seconds. She immediately says, "Hard rock. Rock hard. Oh cool, he turned his life around!" Then, just to add insult to injury, she lays another boot in my midriff and says, "God, I've got to join a gym."

So much creative work is just making it more simple.

People are always relieved to hear something rephrased in a simple way.

If you say too much, you end up saying nothing. "Hard rock. Rock hard." These four words said so much more than my original 600 and the ad was a huge success—all because my creative director killed my babies.

Leaving space for the viewer

That gut kick also exemplified one of the craziest extra benefits of being super simple: it leaves your audience room to draw their own conclusions. It allows them to enter the story, play a role, and in that process, buy in. If you've ever stepped back and let your boss think something was his/her idea, you know the magic. They enter, they become emotionally invested, yours becomes theirs, and they love it. Movies leave spaces open for us all the time; it's one of the reasons their dialogue is so sparse. Filmmaker Jason Wolos puts it really well:

> "Having the audience fill in between the gaps allows them to bring their own world into it, their own issues, their own values, their own morals. It allows them to make that story a little bit more their own."

Showing not telling

As I mentioned earlier, movies use visuals and sound to make everything more real for us, but it also makes the stories more simple. Seeing and hearing the actual characters, action, and setting is so much less work on our brains than having to read it.

It also cuts the amount of time needed to present the story, which is how movies based on books can deliver the story in a fraction of the time it takes us to read it. Take *The Shining*—Steven King's book is 688 pages, but Stanley Kubrick's screenplay is 147. That's because King might have to spend a sentence or even a paragraph describing what something looks like, whereas Kubrick can show it to you in a second and you'll get it even more clearly. And while King has to tell you what his characters are thinking, Jack Nicholson can make you feel it with a quick gesture or voice inflection.

In your work, you can do that as well. For instance, you can show a whole series of demographic stats with one image. Put a man in front of his house people will immediately see his age range, ethnicity and get a good sense of his income and neighborhood. Add his kids and you can define him even more. Add his car and you're able to communicate life circumstances and priorities. And how long would it take for your stakeholders to get all that information? A lot less time than running through all those demographics.

In the next chapter, we'll show you how to be visual so you can further cut the time and brainwork needed to make your points. You won't be able to do it on the level of Stanley Kubrick, but you will be able to deliver a lot more in fewer minutes, keep everyone energized and on the same page, and keep your stakeholders' brainpower ready for the information that really matters.

THE BIG TAKEAWAYS
from this chapter

Everyone wants you to be simple.

So much of being "creative" is actually just being simple.

If you say too much, you end up saying nothing. Four words can say far more than 600, and leaving that space for your audience reels them in and encourages emotional investment.

To get simple, get someone to help you kill your babies, someone not involved with your project who can help pull you out of the weeds.

Showing instead of telling makes it far easier on the people you're presenting to because they won't have to imagine it. And it brings them all together around one visual so they remember it the same way.

Case in Point:
Capital One's Project 10on1

In this book, I'll use three case histories to show you how to apply the movie-storytelling principles in a way that aligns more closely with the decks that you put together every day. All three are completely made up because of our confidentiality protocols at Backstories Studio, but they're meant to be realistic corporate projects, and hopefully similar enough to your projects so you can apply them to your work.

In our first case, pretend you work in the consumer insights department (aka "market research") at Capital One.

Your project is for the innovation division. They have a new concept aimed at Millennials called "10on1." With it, Millennials would not use a plastic credit card; they would use the 10on1 app on their phone to pay at the cash register (like they can today with Apple or Android Pay). But with 10on1, they would also get to choose ten different stores or websites to wrap into their app, and get the same benefits and rewards as that store's card. So they go to Banana Republic with the 10on1 app on their phone, and they get the same 40% discount as the person with the Banana card.

The beauty of this is that Capital One would offer Millennials ten times the rewards of a typical card, but Capital One wouldn't have to pay for any of those rewards.

It would also give Capital One a perfect entry into top retailers currently held by competitors. So it's a win-win-win for the company. There are some big obstacles to overcome, though, before they can get buy-in:

- The investment to develop and market the app will be huge

- Merchants like Banana Republic would have to be enticed into buying all the machinery to accept payment by phone. They might also worry about losing the brand relationship that comes with carrying their card

- Millennials per capita have not been the biggest spenders at brick-and-mortar retail

The innovation department has a plan: if they can show that Millennials will spend, the merchants will go for it. And if they can get the merchants, the company will make the investment.

So it's all about knowing whether or not such an app could unleash Millennial spending and bring merchants and Capital One a good ROI (return on investment). It would, of course, be great to develop a prototype and hand it to a group of Millennials for a pilot study, but that's insanely expensive and in the world of finance, things don't move at lightning speed. So today, it's all about looking at existing ways Millennials can pay with their phones and getting feedback from Millennials on the innovations team's ideas to see if they'll increase their spending.

I know, not nearly as exciting as it could be, but more indicative of everyday work, wouldn't you say? Plus it aligns with our challenge of taking something that might be boring and bringing it to life through visual stories. So stick with me, folks, while I throw you more not-so-exciting news.

You also don't have much budget, so your data is going to come from a survey. Here you'll test the ideas the innovations group has for the Phone-Directed Shopping Experience (PDSE), where as soon as the Millennials walk into a store, the phone will offer them coupons and rewards on the spot. You've designed the survey to work on a phone so Millennial respondents can be in the store when they see the idea mocked up, then indicate if it will entice them to buy or move further toward a purchase. You also have the syndicated research you already subscribe to, like the Futures Company Monitor. It has tons of demographic and psychographic data on Millennials, their buying power, and spending habits.

Okay, ready for some good news?
Your data came back and it all looks really positive. The ideas for 10on1 all spurred spending, and the syndicated research points to this being a promising opportunity.

Unfortunately, you cannot present the findings yourself, because the innovations group has to roadshow it to the key merchants and doesn't have the budget to bring you. Instead, they've asked you to prepare 15 minutes' worth of slides they can incorporate into their presentation.

Ouch! You have to trust someone else to present your slide deck? Even if you walk them through it a hundred times, how can you be sure they'll explain it all correctly?

You can't, but that's how it rolls much of the time, isn't it? The truth, though, is that even if you did get to present it, the merchants would still need to explain it to their teams and stakeholders, so you'd always have to trust it to someone. In other words, your story needs to be strong and simple enough to speak for itself, and do it within 15 minutes.

And right now, you have 100+ pages of data, including:

METHODOLOGY:
- Demographic and psychographic data from syndicated research
- Nationwide survey on appeal of program
  - 1,500 surveyed, 250 have used Android Pay
  - 750 will get PDSE

SYNDICATED RESEARCH:
- Millennials are the largest demographic group
- Millennials have $4.2 billion in disposable income
- Millennials are the most ethnically diverse life stage
- Millennials are highly family oriented
- Millennials feel most optimistic about the future
- Millennials have grown up in booms and busts
- Millennials see themselves as a solution
- Millennials are wary of corporations
- Millennials are digital natives
- Millennials believe technology is the best solution
- Millennials are first adopters of all technology
- Apps top the list of preferred solutions
- Millennials save at a higher rate than other life stages

- Millennials are wary of financial institutions
- Millennials prefer not to invest in stocks and bonds
- Millennials prefer to invest in startups
- Millennials want other financial options
- Millennials value experiences over products
- Story brands vs. product brands
- Millennials seek authenticity
- Millennials spend less on packaged goods
- Millennials are not brand loyal
- Millennials prefer to co-create products with brands
- Feel the industry needs to go that way
- No one is doing it well
- Paying with phone is perceived as valuable
- Paying with phone is perceived as convenient
- Paying with phone is perceived as enjoyable
- Perceived use is high
- Overall appeal is high
- Millennials prefer it over plastic cards
- Millennials see pay-with-phone as the future

SURVEY RESULTS
- Paying with phone is perceived as convenient
- Paying with phone is perceived as enjoyable
- Would spur spontaneous shopping
- Would spur trial of new merchants
- They would use it on food, staples, and discretionary purchases
- They use it an average of 4 times per day
- They select stores that are pay-with-phone enabled
- Security concerns are low
- Privacy concerns are low
- Appreciate merchant messages via app up to four times per week
- Appreciate merchant messages via app while in store - three times per visit
- Appreciate merchant messages via email up to once per week

- Appreciate merchant messages via text up to twice per week
- Would associate positive experience with app brand
- 10on1's PDSE increased purchase intent 37%
- PDSE would lead them to different parts of store
- On-spot couponing is appealing
- On-spot couponing increased consideration
- On-spot reward choice would increase purchase intent
- Paying process perception is high
- Would associate positive experience with merchant brand
- Enhanced brand relationship for merchants
- Enhanced brand associations with payment app brand
- Would recommend to friends
- Want options to incorporate friends
- Would want to co-create rewards
- Top 5 reward suggestions
- Top 5 non-cash reward suggestions

So yes, there's a lot here—way more than 15 minutes. It needs to be culled down to what really matters and then shaped into a story. So let's start with question #1.

What do your stakeholders need to do?

Our stakeholders need to get the green light for further development. To make that happen, they need to instill confidence in merchants and management that the ROI will be there. They need to feel good about the ideas, but more importantly, they have to walk away convinced that the direction is sound.

Now that we know that, let's use that laser focus to inform our answers to question #2.

What are the three most important things they'll need to do it right?

Millennials are numerous and into technology; that's common knowledge. So I think we can leave out most of the syndicated research. Those insights are also consistent with the survey data, which addresses it on a specific pay-with-phone level. So we can lean on the survey or combine them for a one-two punch.

One of the biggest takeaways from the survey, though, is that Millennials see paying with their phones as the inevitable future. Because of their demographic size, this suggests that merchants will need to make the investment at some point anyway, so we can use this fact to show why the ideas are timely.

Hitting that point first will wake up stakeholders and create urgency—when change is inevitable, there's always a race to own the innovation, and no one wants to be left out. So for point number one, let's choose:

1. Millennials see pay-with-phone as the future.

Key point #2

Now that we've woken them up and spiked their blood pressure with the notion of a huge investment, it makes sense to turn around and relax them by letting them know that their ROI is looking good. Many of the data points suggest that Millennials will spend more if they can pay with their phones.

This is especially true of the features Capital One envisions for 10on1, like the special custom-tailored discounts Millennials can get when they walk up to the item and scan the tag. The data points not only show appeal, but suggest they'll buy even more if their phone is more than just a payment device.

Emotions are a very real dynamic in the conference room.

Anything new is a stretch. And every stretch eventually needs to be relaxed.

But hitting this point also does something else. It gives the merchants a way to gain back some of the control they fear they're losing. Remember, we just told them Millennials wouldn't be carrying around their cards anymore, but instead would be using their own devices. Having a way to direct those devices will give merchants a feeling of command. Yes, this is completely emotional, but as I'm sure you've experienced, emotions are a very real dynamic in the conference room. Because it's not yet offered, it's also a point of difference that Capital One can develop. So for point number two, what do you say we choose:

2. 10on1's PDSE will increase purchase intent by 37%.

Key point #3
Now down to our last point. As exciting as it is to show more potential, I believe you always get further by mitigating risks, especially when asking for new investments. Because no matter how much you wow them with your idea, fear is this relentless beast that always seems to come back after your presentation is done. I'm sure you know what I'm talking about. When you don't hear back within a week or so...when they say they need more time to consider...that's when they're mulling over the risks of your initiative, and rarely do we ever get to be a voice in that room.

So for our final point, I suggest we tackle merchants' other big worry: losing the relationship that comes with a customer having a store card. Again, we're really lucky that the data give us some good news. It also helps that

the new product team thought this one through and plans to suggest that the merchant's logo be featured on the receipt screen.

3. Enhances brand relationship

Now we have all three key points and the makings of a clear, compelling story that shows potential and also mitigates fears. Millennials see paying by phones as inevitable, but they'll also spend more, especially when we direct them, and yes, merchants, they'll still love you.

Now let's pick the rest of our slides
For our 15 minutes, how many slides do you think we'll need? Well, think about how long you normally spend on a slide? Two or three minutes? If so, you're about average, and that will give you about five or six slides.

Anyone else feeling anxious about cutting close to 70 slides down to five or six? I would be too. I'm not sure I'll be able to tell a rich and credible story with just five slides. So how about instead of spending two to three minutes on each slide, we spend just one minute per slide so we can have 15 slides instead of five? Sound good?

To be that quick, we'll need to take a few cues from the movies. We'll need to be more simple with each slide and recall what we did to that Glenn Frey ad. Go from 600 words down to just four. In other words, we have to do some serious editing.

First, we'll do it on the deck level to get to 15, then we'll do it on the slide level to get each down to one minute or less. To help us, I'm going to bring in a very special guest.

Ladies and gentlemen, filmmaker David Mamet
David Mamet is a legend in film and theater. He's written and directed dozens of movies and plays, including *Glengarry Glen Ross* with Alec Baldwin. Remember: "First place is a Cadillac El Dorado, second place is a set of steak knives, third place is...you're fired!" That was classic Mamet, a man so ruthless, he can kill his own babies. He'll help us cull our slide count down to 15, no problem.

Mamet uses a technique that will help you simplify this deck. When reviewing a script, he takes each of his scenes individually and pulls them out. Then he looks at the scene before it and the one after and asks himself if the story works without the scene he just pulled out. If it doesn't work, the scene stays in, but if the story can survive without it—straight into the trash it goes.

In our deck, we have lots of recyclables. Most of our syndicated research can be tossed. We needed it to get up to speed, but that's because we needed to develop the story. Our stakeholders don't need nearly as much information, and frankly, don't want it. It's not math class, so we don't have to show our work. They just want the answer, and in a way they can believe.

On the next page you'll see the slide list again. The slides Mamet and I recommend tossing are in red. The key slides are underlined. Just like in films, we'll give more focus to those key scenes so we can create moments that grab stakeholders and make them savor the thought. We'll design those slides differently, so stakeholders will know these are key moments.

Presentations, especially to execs at your own company, are not math class.

They don't want to see how you got to the answers, they just want the answers themselves.

■ TOSSERS   ■ KEEPERS

METHODOLOGY:
- Demographic and psychographic data from syndicated research
- Nationwide survey on appeal of program
  - 1500 surveyed, 750 with 10on1 features

SYNDICATED RESEARCH
- Millennials are the largest demographic group
- Millennials have $4.2 billion in disposable income
- Millennials are the most ethnically diverse life stage
- Millennials are highly family oriented
- Millennials feel most optimistic about the future
- Millennials have grown up in booms and busts
- Millennials see themselves as a solution
- Millennials are wary of corporations
- Millennials are digital natives
- Millennials believe technology is the best solution
- Millennials are first adopters of all technology
- Apps top the list of preferred solutions
- Millennials save at a higher rate than other life stages
- Millennials are wary of financial institutions
- Millennials prefer not to invest in stocks and bonds
- Millennials prefer to invest in startups
- Millennials want other financial options
- Millennials value experiences over products
- Story brands vs. product brands
- Millennials seek authenticity
- Millennials spend less on packaged goods
- Millennials are not brand loyal
- Millennials prefer to co-create products with brands
- Feel the industry needs to go that way
- No one is doing it well
- Paying with phone is perceived as valuable
- Paying with phone is perceived as convenient
- Paying with phone is perceived as enjoyable
- Perceived use is high
- Overall appeal is high
- Millennials prefer it over plastic cards
- Millennials see pay-with-phone as the future

SURVEY RESULTS
- Paying with phone is perceived as convenient
- Paying with phone is perceived as enjoyable
- Would spur spontaneous shopping
- Would spur trial of new merchants
- They would use it on food, staples and discretionary purchases
- They use it an average of 4 times per day
- They select stores that are pay-with-phone enabled
- Security concerns are low
- Privacy concerns are low
- Appreciate merchant messages via app ≥ 4/week
- Appreciate merchant messages via app while in store - up to 3 per visit
- Appreciate merchant messages via email up to 1 per week
- Appreciate merchant messages via text up to 2 per week
- Would associate positive experience with app brand
- PDSE increased purchase intent 37%
- PDSE would lead them to different parts of store
- On-spot couponing is appealing
- On-spot couponing increased consideration
- On-spot reward choice would increase purchase intent
- Paying process perception is high
- Would associate positive experience with merchant brand
- Enhanced brand relationship for merchants
- Enhanced brand associations with payment app brand
- Would recommend to friends
- Want options to incorporate friends
- Would want to co-create rewards
- Top 5 reward suggestions
- Top 5 non-cash reward suggestions

How I chose my 15

It's all about supporting the three big points and cutting out slides that don't drive to them. For example, since we're taking this to merchants, I jettisoned the slides about Capital One's brand because merchants won't care. When it gets presented to internal management, I'll put those back in.

Other choices are about looking at a group of related slides and picking the one that says it best, like including "on-spot couponing increases consideration," over the previous slide about appeal. If it increases consideration, it's obviously appealing.

Others, like these first two below, are about managing the political climate in the room.

1.   But will it turn Millennials into loyal buyers?
2.   Nationwide survey on appeal of program
      • 1500 surveyed, 750 with 10on1

My first slide is a new, introductory concept: the central business question. This shows empathy for their big concerns and lets them know we're not wasting their time. Similarly, the methodology slide establishes our credibility. For an internal audience, I wouldn't bother with the methodology. Most stakeholders, especially execs, figure that if you're in the room, you're trustworthy. But this is an external audience being asked to take a leap into Anxietyland, so I want them to know I didn't just pull this out of thin air.

I chose the first three points below ("convenient," "enjoyable," and "prefer it over plastic cards") because they're more concrete than "perceived as valuable." They're more specific, and thus easier for stakeholders to grasp.

I also moved "convenient" and "enjoyable" to the front because they're easy concepts to warm up the group, and more importantly, they'll set up my first big point of "Millennials see pay-with-phone as the future."

3.   Paying with phone is perceived as convenient
4.   Paying with phone is perceived as enjoyable
5.   Millennials prefer it over plastic cards
6.   <u>Millennials see pay-with-phone as the future</u>

The rest of the slides I chose for similar reasons. They hit their points more concretely than the others around them, and do a good job of driving toward the key points.

7.   Would spur spontaneous shopping
8.   They use it an average of 4 times per day
9.   But the data show a way to ratchet the potential even further
10. On-spot couponing increased item visits
11. On-spot reward choice increased consideration
12. <u>PDSE increased purchase intent 37%</u>
13. Would recommend to friends
14. But what about the merchant brand?
15. <u>Enhanced brand relationship for merchants</u>

OUR ORIGINAL SLIDE

2-3 minutes to present

Probably 4 minutes to read on your own

But who knows how long to understand?

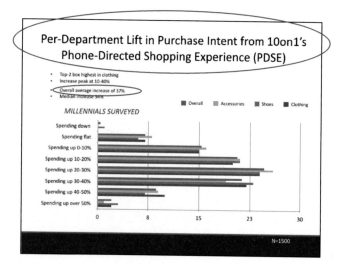

Simplifying each slide

Now, as promised, we've got to get the slides down to something that can be presented in a minute or less. That's a lot easier than you'd imagine because no matter how complicated a chart is, there's usually only one big point you want to make. Maybe two, but usually only one, right?

For instance, in the case of the slide to the left, the point we want to make is: when we added the 10on1's PDSE to the test, it raised purchase intent 37% throughout the store. There are two areas on the chart that point to that. I've ovaled them in red.

Everything else on the slide just hides that key point and the clutter illustrates why the slide would take so long to present, because you'll need to be one of those CSI detectives that shows everyone the big clues, then puts the whole picture together.

That's great in the room, because it gives you a key role in the presentation, but again, what happens when you're not there to help them through the muck? When your stakeholders need to show the slide to their bosses or teams?

Unfortunately, when they no longer have the expert guide to lead them through the weeds, chances are they won't be able to do the detective work themselves and show everyone the real point. They'll read the headline and get most of it, but then when they point to the chart, they'll have to struggle to find the data point that backs it up. That makes it really hard to evoke credibility and doesn't do much for anyone's confidence.

So instead, what if we cut out all that clutter, killed all the babies in the weeds, and just brought out what really matters—big and bold for everyone to see and believe. And what if we further simplified it by not revealing the "+37%" right away? Spaced out the information into bite-sized chunks like movies do. Maybe even phrased it as a question to set up our little cliffhanger drama:

"So what was 10on1's phone-directed shopping experience effect on purchase intent?"

Then wait...then reveal...."It raised it 37%.

Wouldn't creating that moment make a huge difference in impact? Wouldn't the slide on the right be so much easier on your stakeholders' eyes and brains? Wouldn't it be easier for them to remember and relay its point to their bosses and teams?

If you agree, awesome. Because if all you do is simplify your slides and get rid of the "Same What?" you'll be leaps and bounds ahead of everyone else firehosing their stakeholders with too much data.

That said, wait until you see what we do in the next chapter with these 15 little data diamonds in the rough.

OUR SIMPLIFIED SLIDE

Seconds to present

Seconds to read on your own

Seconds to understand

10on1's PDSE raised purchase intent 37%

CHAPTER 3

Make It Real

with context that takes them right there

Now that I've sufficiently beaten you over the head with the concept of simplicity, I'm going to throw a monkey wrench at you with this caveat: sometimes you can be <u>too</u> simple.

Consultants are often guilty of this. They come to you with recommendations like, "You have to create an experience," "It's all about trust," or my favorite, "Be authentic." Those axioms are lovely, but they're also just as abstract as charts and just as difficult for stakeholders to put into action. They just sound sexy, and because they often come from consultants, they're usually really expensive.

To put them in story terms: they are themes, but for themes to mean anything, they need to be put into context with some more-basic story elements: characters, settings, and action. These basic ingredients give us the context we need to visualize, understand, and relate to a concept. "Something happens to somebody somewhere." Give us that and we can see it, or at least imagine it. Then it becomes real enough to work with. And even more important, real enough to start caring about.

Let me give you an example. I'll play Mr. Pithy Consultant. My recommendation/theme is "appreciation." We all know what that means, right? Or do we? Let me ask you this: are you even remotely beginning to care? Probably not, so let me re-frame it with some real movie-style context.

Settings

Let's start with a setting. Actually, let's make it two: Kansas and Oz. (Gee, wherever could he be going with this?) But let's look at those two settings, Kansas and Oz, in terms of appreciation. Kansas is where Dorothy feels unappreciated and, in turn, doesn't appreciate anything or anyone either. But as soon as she lands in Oz, what happens? Dorothy is given instant appreciation and treated like Munchkin royalty. And to accentuate that flip for viewers, the filmmakers applied a handy little tool called "contrast" to the settings to emulate Dorothy's experience. Kansas = dull black and white; Oz = colorful, bright, and cheery. So just in the settings, and the contrast between them,

we immediately feel that emotional shift that Dorothy feels, and are set up right alongside Dorothy to learn about appreciation.

Characters

Now let's introduce some characters, because that's when it really gets engaging: Dorothy is, of course, our hero, so her role is to carry the message of appreciation. She's our guide. Throughout the story, we'll experience everything Dorothy experiences and feel what she feels, so in the end, we'll have learned about appreciation the same ways she does.

The next main character is the Wicked Witch. In movie terms, she's the "opponent." The reason I didn't say "villain" is because not all stories have villains. For instance, in any love story, the opponent is the hero's love interest. In buddy pictures, it's the buddy. The thing these archetypes have in common is their role in pushing and prodding the heroes to learn what they need to learn and do what they need to do to become heroic. Whether it's Ilsa from *Casablanca*, who forces Rick to find his soul, or the Wicked Witch, who throws so many flying monkeys at Dorothy that she finally transcends the helpless little woe-is-me girl into real maturity, the opponents are there to make the heroes dig deep, find courage and strength, and take risks that they never would on their own.

Here's the best part: you can be the opponent that makes your stakeholders heroic. If you have an initiative, recommendations, or news that isn't a slam dunk,

A TALE TOLD WITH CONTRAST

The filmmakers of The Wizard of Oz *wanted to make it Technicolor-clear how different Dorothy's worlds were.*

chances are your stakeholders will need to incur some risk before giving you buy-in, and definitely afterward. They too may need to dig deep to find their courage and strength. We'll talk at length in the second section of this book on how we'll prep them for those battles, but by the end of this chapter, you'll have the most important thing they'll need: a clear way for them to retell your story once your presentation is delivered.

The last main character in our example is the Wizard. In filmland he's called the Sage. The Sage also helps the hero find strength, but the more important role is to provide understanding. Obi-Wan Kenobi is another good example of a Sage. Yoda is usually thought of as the Sage, but Obi-Wan does something that's also relevant to your job: he pops in to give Luke advice when he needs it most—like the turning-point scene in the X-wing fighter when he tells Luke to "use the Force." One of the key ways you can elevate your relationship with your stakeholders and get a seat at the table is to check in with them from time to time and offer perspective and solutions. Doing so really lets them know you're thinking big picture and enhancing value.

Plot

The plot is the sequence of action that makes the story work. It's similar to a "narrative," but has more design to it. A narrative is just how the story gets from the beginning to the end. A plot is how you strategize that narrative so it has emotional power. Like holding back certain information until key moments, or mapping out a character's emotional journey so it has more impact. It's what takes a story from merely informational to something gripping. Sorry to keep saying we'll go more in depth in future chapters, but we will, because our whole section on high-stakes presentations is about being as gripping and impactful as possible.

The plot of *The Wizard of Oz* is:

Dorothy makes it out of Kansas.

Dorothy lands in Oz.

Dorothy saves Oz from the Wicked Witch.

Dorothy meets the Wizard, and then …

Dorothy realizes something.

Do you remember what she realizes? Yep, that's right: "There's no place like home." In other words: our theme. She finally realizes that in order to feel appreciated, she too has to appreciate.

Do you remember the first time you heard "There's no place like home"? Did it make you sigh or tear up, or at least look over at your annoying brother with a warm, cuddly feeling? That's the power of context. Those "basic" story elements—settings, characters, and plot—have the real ability to mess with your mind and heart and make your theme more powerful and emotionally moving—certainly more than when I wrote "appreciation" a few pages ago. I don't think there's any way a high-priced consultant would have made you think warmly about your brother by merely recommending "appreciation." But add context and you'll forgive 1,000 noogies.

The green curtain that is data

Do you remember where we meet the Wizard when Dorothy is brought into the Emerald City and sees that big head yelling at her?

Yep, he's behind the curtain.

I think another reason why charts are so prevalent in business presentations is that they can be a curtain for us to hide behind. We think that as long as we present the data, those stats can speak for themselves: factual, quantified, validated, done.

Unfortunately, the truth is a bit more harsh: we're just like the Wizard. And just as Dorothy couldn't connect with him until he came out from behind the curtain, we won't be able to connect with our stakeholders until we do the same thing.

I'm now going to bring in my own sage/wizard. Nancy Duarte leads the most successful presentation design firm in the U.S., Duarte Design. In her book, *Slide:ology* (far and away the best book on PowerPoint-style presentations that I've seen), she says:

"Data slides are not about the data. They're about the meaning of the data."

That meaning comes from adding context. Context will lift your curtain, connect your stakeholders to the data, and get you and your information heard.

Characters are your guides

I think the easiest way to find that context is to identify your characters. They will lead you to your story. The characters in your data might be consumers your data are capturing. Or if your data reveal an opportunity, the characters might be the people who can capitalize on it, like your colleagues who can use the information to start innovating. Every piece of data involves someone or something (products and brands can also be characters). They're either being described or being empowered. Often it's both, and that's where you can double down on your meaning.

I know, I'm probably still sounding fuzzy. But fear not—there are two words you use all the time that can help you find your characters; and as a bonus, your setting and plot.

Go get yourself a piece of data right now and examine it long enough to get the key takeaway in your head. Ready? Now say to yourself:

For example _____

When you filled in the rest of that sentence, I'll bet some characters, setting, and a simple plot popped into your head. If they didn't, spend a little more time with your data point so you really understand its meaning and try again. You'll soon have your characters, your context, and a way for your stakeholders to understand your data more easily.

"Data slides are not about the data. They're about the meaning of the data."

- Nancy Duarte

Don't stop there

Now let's be even more meaningful for your stake-holders and extend our Madlib so you're not only giving them the context of your data point, but also the context they will need to capitalize on it. It's that "so what...?" that so many execs are looking for. You can find it with just the word "so____."

Go back to your data point again, imagine you're saying it to your key stakeholder, and repeat after me:

For example _____,

so _____.

Did a conclusion or opportunity pop into your head? If so, you've just made your data even more meaningful by showing your stakeholders how they can apply it. That not only helps them out, but will also keep the integrity of your data intact by making it easier to follow your thinking. The chances of them misconstruing it are reduced now that they can now see how it applies to them and how they can use it.

Time to back myself up and give you a meaningful example. We're going to do a bit of what we did in the last chapter—make a chart more simple—but then we're going to take it even further by adding context and laying it out as a simple movie-style story.

Imagine that you work for CB Home or one of the other big real estate brokerages. You're presenting to realtors at the branch-office level on how to sell more houses. Take a look at the slide on the right and tell me your key takeaway.

If you're frustrated, don't feel bad. Whenever I show this slide in my workshops, no one gets it, even after a full minute. And this is very close to an actual slide I pulled from one of those big realty companies.

The key takeaway the realtors will need from this slide can be found by linking these items:

- you can lift the interest and emotional investment
- of buyers at open houses
- mostly by talking about holidays
- and dogs

Why was that so hard? Well, just like the slide in our previous chapter, it's not the data, it's the clutter-fest of the layout. It makes you look in four different places and construct the story on your own. Then it makes it even harder by hiding those four key things within a bunch of information that isn't going to help our realtors.

It's true that when you present in person, you can guide people through the slide, but again, it really pays to think about when you can't be there to do it for them—like when your stakeholders share your deck with their teams.

OUR CHART BEFORE

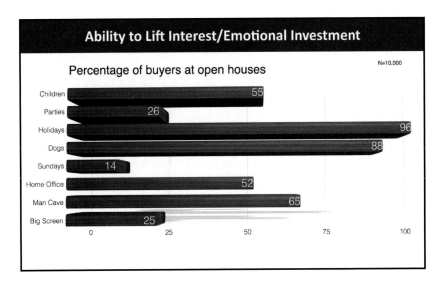

Ability to Lift Interest/Emotional Investment

Percentage of buyers at open houses

N=10,000

Children	55
Parties	26
Holidays	96
Dogs	88
Sundays	14
Home Office	52
Man Cave	65
Big Screen	25

0   25   50   75   100

Time to give our chart the movie-style treatment

Let's now approach our chart a different way, one that uses those three elements of context (setting, characters, plot), our movie principles of being simple, linear, and visual, and our "so" that puts it in the realtors' context.

But first, let's start with the Big2 questions so we make sure it's relevant for our stakeholders—the realtors you're presenting to:

<u>What do they need to do?</u> Sell more houses

<u>What information will help them do it right</u>? Emotionally resonant topics they can mention when buyers come to their open house.

Back on the last page, we identified the key data. Now let's construct our story to include the characters, setting, and action that makes it clear, and also the "so" that will make it actionable for our realtors. Here are our building blocks:

<u>Characters</u>: buyers and realtors

<u>Setting</u>: open house

<u>Plot</u>: emotional attachment gets lifted by mentioning holidays and dogs

<u>So</u>: Realtors can bring up these topics with buyers and evoke that emotional attachment that naturally will lead to more offers.

What are the best topics realtors can mention so buyers will feel attached to their open house?

96% say Holidays

78% say Dogs

Now take a look at the slide above. It has the same key information, but isn't this slide easier to understand than the first version? What's more, if you saw it onscreen, built one point at a time, it would be even easier to get because we can steal the movie principle of laying out the story one piece of information at a time. The whole thing takes four clicks:

Click 1: What are the best topics realtors can mention so buyers will feel attached to their open house?

Click 2: 96% say holidays.

Click 3: 78% say dogs.

Click 4: Enter Puppy Claus.

Here are some other techniques I used to make it even more effective:

I phrased the headline as a question to give my audience room to participate—the same way I left out the text in the Glenn Frey ad.

I held back the answers to that question to build anticipation for the next click, and drive my story toward my key point, rather than from it. This also heightened the simplicity by giving information one piece at a time.

Then I brought in Puppy Claus to make it visually memorable and cement the love. I also chose Puppy Claus because every promotional piece I've ever seen from a realtor is super cheesy, so it enabled me to go further into their context by speaking their visual language.

Now before I lose you to puppy cuteness overload, think about this: the data points from the cluttered slide that I did not include: did you miss them? Feel free to look back.

It may not be a movie, but all the techniques I employed are used in movies every day. And most importantly, if you're a realtor, you're no longer bored. Your eyes just got super wide and your ears just perked up because I called your name and brought you an opportunity. It's in your world now and you know just what to do. That, my friends, is the magic of context.

THE BIG TAKEAWAYS
from this chapter

Without context, any topic is difficult to understand. Buzz phrases like "make it authentic" or "create an experience" go nowhere without giving people context.

The same is true for data. Data points are meaningless without context, so don't think that all you have to do is present them.

To find context in anything, find the characters. They can be the people or things your data point is depicting or the people who can jump on the opportunity your data presents.

Once you find the characters, put them in a setting and bring them to life with some action so everyone can picture it.

Once you've got your basic story, put your stakeholder hat on so you can understand it from their perspective. Ask the question "so___?" and fill in the blank. Now retune your story to offer even more meaning.

Back to our Case in Point:
Capital One's Project "10on1"

When last we left our 10on1 project, where we surveyed Millennials on their behaviors and attitudes about paying with their phones, we killed many babies and got our deck down to 15 slides. We also simplified one of our slides so it could be explained in less than one minute, helping our colleagues present the key parts of our findings in their slim time slot without messing it up (hopefully). How cool are we?

Here, again, is the before and after versions of our slide. Gone from the "after" is the information that doesn't matter to the merchants. Now they can clearly see how much 10on1 will raise purchase intent.

But does our "after" slide tell much of a story? Can you see or feel what's going on? Will you be able to remember it? Not really—it's actually pretty forgettable, and if we laid out our other 14 slides in the same simple way, it would also be difficult to distinguish from the others. So even though it's much easier to understand than our "before" slide, we still won't be giving our merchant stakeholders enough to hold their attention and buy into our colleagues' ideas for 10on1.

So let's put in some context and bring these guys to life. What do we need for that? Settings, characters, and action.

Our characters are Millennials, our setting is a retail store, and our action is the 10on1 app guiding their shopping experience. The good news is that all of those things are easily found, probably within a few miles of where we work or live.

Before

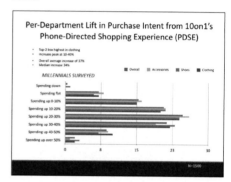

After

So first: characters. Let's find ourselves a Millennial. That's actually pretty easy. You probably have several sitting right in your office who could model for you. Or better yet, let's go a route which requires no favors or lunches: run an ad in the modeling gigs section on craigslist.org. Our ad can be as simple as this:

20-something for 2-hour shoot
Male or female model in his/her 20s needed for 2-hour photo shoot where we'll capture you shopping and buying items on a phone (we'll supply the phone, but you must know how to use an iPhone).

$150. If interested, please send photos.

See? Nothing fancy. In fact, I recommend not getting fancy so the model will not expect a high-end shoot. This will take the pressure off you, which is really important since you don't do this every day.

Within a day we receive 114 inquiries (a typical Craigslist response). We hear from men, women, people of all kinds of ethnicities, wearing all kinds of outfits and expressions. We receive responses from agents representing professional models as well as photos so blurry we can't tell who we're looking at. We want someone in the middle, though: attractive but real, like a person we can see in one of the merchants' stores.

That helps us cull it down to 20 people. We then respond back with the dates that work for us. We also reiterate the pay and what we want our model to do so it's crystal-clear. That gets us down to five people and from them, we chose Sophia because she just seems to most closely fit our vision. We then exchange a few more logistical emails, ask her to bring a few outfits, but nothing outside her regular range. In fact, we tell her we don't want anything that will draw too much attention because we want her and the action to be the star.

The fun starts

The day before the shoot, we look back at our 15 slides and think about which setting and action might work best to bring them to life. We then take a walk through the retail sections of downtown to scout locations. We expense lunch, a cup of fancy coffee, and take notes. More importantly, we take our time so we'll feel confident tomorrow and have an easier shoot.

We also choose a camera. I have fancier ones, but for this shoot we chose my cheapest camera, a Canon Digital Rebel, for two reasons. First, we're not going to be able to get permission to shoot in the mall, so we'll need something that doesn't look even remotely professional. And second, the real-life reason (sorry to break out of character): when I took the actual photos I'm using in this make-believe story, that was the camera I used. Today, I have an even better choice that I would use instead: the Sony Cybershot RX100. It takes great photos and has tons of controls, but is really easy to use and draws even less attention to itself than the Rebel. There it is on the right.

Anyway, back to our make-believe case history:

Semi-professional without the fuss

We set the camera on the highest resolution and on "Av," or aperture priority, so we can open up the iris as much as possible. On the Sony, that's 1.8, which is why it's such a good camera. A low aperture number like 1.8 means that you can let in a ton of light. That makes your shots look better, lets you manage all kinds of conditions, and also allows you to blur your background, which looks far more professional than if you shot the photo on your phone. Having that blurred background also makes your picture more simple because everyone's eye is immediately locked into what's in focus. That's a big movie trick you see in closeups. Everything else is completely out of focus so you'll look at what the filmmakers want you to look at.

Choosing this focus point, though, comes with one hitch: if you're not focusing on a face, you may need to manually focus your camera by hand because you cannot use face-detection auto-focus. Don't worry. Focusing manually is not nearly as difficult as it sounds. It takes practice, but if you take your time—an extra five or ten seconds per shot—you'll be able to get detail shots of hands and objects and scenes that the auto focus can't always get (although auto focus seems to be getting smarter and smarter every day).

We shoot up the town

Sophia arrives and she's really nice. She doesn't care that we're not professional photographers and appreciates that we're not trying to act like we are. She lays her outfits on the conference room table and we choose the one that feels best for the slides and the weather outside.

Because we'd scouted locations the day before, we know which stores and restaurants will best match our slides. We've also installed screenshot comps of the 10on1 ideas that were on the survey, as well as the two payment services our Millennials in the survey had, Android Pay and Google Wallet. Finally, we installed the Starbucks app which allows pay-with-phone so we can start with a cup of coffee (gotta get fueled up, right?). We then hand the phone to Sophia so she can use it for the next couple of hours.

We take a few portraits of Sophia using the phone in the office, and then we hit the streets. First, we grab our coffee, then we go to the stores we scouted and take pictures of Sophia using the phone in all the ways described in our 15 slides. We also take many more, in case we need to give our stakeholders more slides later. And we're having a great time, so why not?

Framing them up makes it easier for you

Whenever we frame up a shot, we pull out a printout of the slide it's intended for. That helps us figure out what action we want to shoot, and also how to frame it so we can accommodate the text and numbers we also want on the slide. That means we shouldn't put Sophia's face or our visual point in the center of the photo. We need to reserve some space for our stat and information.

Generally, our headline and stat are going to be on the left side, so we keep that open and put Sophia on the right side of the frame. We also try to keep Sophia's body and face turned toward the number so it will draw stakeholders toward it. And we try to keep some distance between Sophia and the background so that area will end up blurry, and not distract too much from the stat. The picture on the right illustrates what I mean. Ideally, we'd also like to keep that area dark, but we'll do what we can.

What makes it even easier

I've been on dozens of photo shoots and one thing that all professional photographers do, especially now that most are on digital cameras, is take far more photos than they need. They know they can always edit them down, but won't be able to recreate the shoot very easily if they discover that they don't have enough shots. And also because, like the rest of us, sometimes they mess up. Blurred shots, dark shots, bad shots: professionals shoot them all. But it's okay, because they know as long as they get the shot they need, it doesn't matter if they have to shoot ten terrible ones to get it. Photography is the opposite of presentation decks: there's quality in quantity and allowing yourself to do those ten terrible shots is part of the process.

The Sony Cybershot RX100 is the camera I use when I need to be stealthy in public (for example, a shopping mall).

Here's Sophia in the mall. I kept her on the right side of the frame so I could put my information in the open space on the left.

Professional photographers take about 100 shots to get that one good one. So don't pressure yourself to be Ansel Adams on every shot. Have fun, shoot away, and edit later.

I say this because, just like taking your time when you scout your settings, make sure you plan enough time to leisurely go through your shoot. Take your time so you can get your shot, then—just like a professional photographer—line up a bunch of variations you may or may not need. Explore all your ideas, explore suggestions your model offers, and shoot, shoot, shoot away. You might think your model will mind, but he/she won't. If you're having fun and within the time frame you agreed to, it will still be the easiest money they've made all week. And you'll have fun and feel great—way better than being back at your desk.

But back to our story:

So we take our time with Sophia, enjoy our afternoon, take about 300 snaps (some godawful) to get our 15, and finish in just about two hours.

We then have her sign a release that grants us permission to use the photos of her. Again, no need to be fancy; our release is two simple sentences. We give her $150 and wave goodbye.

When we get back

After we choose our favorites, we simply insert our photos into the PowerPoint slides. Because we had that open space in my framing, it goes really easily. Sometimes a shot doesn't work, but because we took so many, we just pick another. Sometimes we have to stretch a photo, but that's fine because we have plenty of resolution. Sometimes we have to shift our headline and stats up or down, but for the most part, we can keep them in a logical and consistent place.

We then show it to our stakeholders. They're absolutely thrilled. No one has ever given them anything like this. They have input, of course (who doesn't?), but also some good ideas that lead us to choose different photos from our shoot. One wacky thing is that it doesn't always matter if our photo isn't showing the actual event suggested by the stat; just having the characters, setting, and action is enough to place our stakeholders in the scene.

Ordering the slides for maximum impact

Earlier I talked about how movies place more emphasis on the key scenes. We want to do that as well by making our key scenes stand out. Our key slides will not have Sophia visuals like the rest. That will also enable us to make the text and numbers bigger, and thus, make a dramatic statement: these are different, these are important.

I also talked about how a movie's scenes in between the key scenes have one job: to drive you to the next key scene. We're going to let our in-between slides do the same thing: drive us to that next key slide. As mentioned in Chapters 1 and 2, this little flip is going to give us a Hollywood weapon that will keep our stakeholders engaged, make our 15-minute presentation feel like five, and make our key points hit even harder because we've built up our stakeholders' anticipation.

I've talked about how anticipation keeps us on the edge of our seats in movies, but we can also learn from a master in the corporate world. When Steve Jobs would present the new Apple product, he would never do it at the beginning of his speech, even though everyone knew that was what he was onstage to do. Instead, he reeled in audiences through anticipation, then delivered the big hit.

I know, a lot of execs say they want you to present the key slides first, then support them. And if your information is super simple, then I would definitely go that way. But the reason they make that request is because they're expecting you to be boring, and they need to give themselves a way to safely drift off if they do get bored.

But that isn't what they really want. They want—and need—the information that supports your recommendations. They just don't want the boring firehose. But by being simple, visual, and evocative, you're not giving them that, so they won't mind.

You're giving them Sophia and that subtle but powerful flip builds anticipation, and makes the time fly by. Speaking of which, here's how we'll lay out our slide story...

A lot of execs say they want you to present the key slides first, and if your information is straightforward, that's the way to go.

But I believe they also say that because they expect you to bore them, so they need a way to manage it.

MILLENNIALS AND THE POTENTIAL OF PAY-WITH-PHONE

Here's how our insights story laid out. It includes two last-minute design changes (I'm always trying to be real). Because the PDSE will have already been thoroughly discussed, we were able to make our original slide (#12) even more simple. And though we wanted slide #15 to stand out like the other key slides, the innovations group thought it would be best to show how the merchant's imagery pops up in the phone app. They know the merchants, so we'll defer to them.

1

In our opening slide, we'll ask the big question to show our empathy for our merchant's main concern.

2

Then we'll hit the methodology to establish our credibility and put questions to rest.

3

Then ease them into it with our first group of insights. No surprise there.

4

Then we'll give them another easy one, and again reinforce it with some positive elaboration.

5

Next we'll get into the first point of controversy, but one that's still pretty expected.

6

Then we'll hit something they won't expect, key point #1. We'll do it in big letters, emphasizing importance and upping urgency. But as the last click, we'll add "however...," to build anticipation.

7

Now that we've set ourselves up with anticipation, we'll give them the first piece of exciting news—a tangible upside: store visits.

8

To reinforce it, we'll show some evidence that it's habitual. Millennials can be enticed to spend. Yes!

9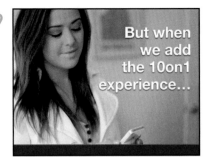

And just when they're excited, we'll create some anticipation for 10on1's key features.

10

Like how well 10on1 did with their first in-store obstacle: getting Millennials to the item.

11

We'll then follow up with showing the rise in consideration, the second big hoop they want shoppers to go through.

12

10on1 raised purchase intent 37%

Now we'll hit them with key point #2. This should be pretty good music to their ears. For if a non-working concept scores this high, just imagine what a real one would do.

13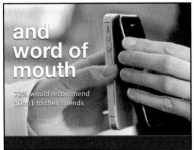

Then we'll bask in the glow a bit and share another big point: recommendation.

14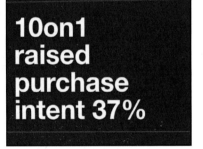

Finally, we'll set up for our final point...

15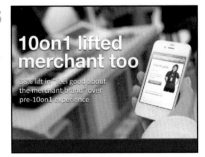

...and end it with our final piece of good news.

2 | WHEN THE STAKES ARE HIGH

It might be once a year or every quarter...

Those times when a big opportunity, money, jobs, or politics are on the line and you have to deliver just as big.

For those times, this is your section.

CHAPTER 4

Make It Powerful

by evoking emotion and all that comes with it

In the past few chapters, we took what could have been a long data deck and turned it into a story that was concise, visual, engaging, and full of meaning. It gave stakeholders exactly what they needed and made the experience easy to learn, and memorable enough to relay to their teams and stakeholders. It was perfect for the kinds of presentations and decks you probably do regularly.

Now it's time to take it further.

Because I'll bet a few times a year, you have a presentation with far higher stakes. One where you really need to hit it out of the park. In this chapter, we'll set you up with the most powerful tool movies have in their box: emotion. Once we add emotion to the mix of everything we've learned so far, all those concepts—simplicity, context, etc.—will gain super-duper-whooper strength. You'll be even more clear and engaging, and you'll inspire and motivate. You may even draw tears, and you'll certainly persuade your stakeholders to take (or approve) action and help you move the business. Because emotion is the magic potion that moves us to decision and action.

THE RATIONAL
CAN STEER

but the
emotional
decides if you go anywhere

We know this is true of consumers—even for their biggest, most important, highest-involvement decisions. Take cars, for example. If people used their rational minds, few would ever buy an SUV. They'd rent one when they went up to the mountains, and buy something more practical for their everyday commute. But they don't do that, because no one follows their rational side. Once the visions of ourselves camping and skiing dance in our heads, any pro-and-con list we made or numbers we crunched just don't stand a chance.

And yet when it comes to our business, we forget about the emotional and speak almost exclusively to the rational sides of our stakeholders' brains. Again, I think it's those bullets and charts on the templates, leading us toward the rational and logical, and away from emotion.

But business people are just as affected by emotion as consumers. Their ways of expressing it might be a little different, but they're still driven by emotion.

For instance, when someone interrupts your presentation by saying, "I need more data on this," it sounds like they're asking for something rational, right? And on the surface, they certainly are. But I'll bet what that stakeholder is really telling you is "If I buy into this, I'm still a little scared my boss is going to have my ass, so I need you to help me cover it."

So even though the request is for rational data, what he really wants is emotional reassurance, and in truth, there may be more effective ways to provide that. In most of the corporations I've been in, an endorsement by an expert or an exec covers a lot more ass than statistical minutiae.

One of my favorite books on framing information is *Switch* by Chip and Dan Heath. *Switch* features a perfect metaphor for the relationship between the rational and the emotional that they found in a book called *The Happiness Hypothesis* by Jonathan Haidt. You'll see the metaphor pictured on the left. It goes like this: Our rational mind is like a human driver, riding on top of our emotional mind, an elephant. The driver (rational mind) gives direction and has these ropes to steer the emotional. But here's the thing: when you really look at the size, strength, and position of these two creatures, let's be honest—who's really going to decide if they go anywhere? It's the same as our brains: informing the rational side of the brain is perfect for giving your stakeholders the facts and tools they need, but to get them to actually do something, they also need to care. They need to be inspired. They need to believe in what you're saying. They need to feel emotion.

Emotion also heightens our ability to understand. Consider the difference between what you've learned from lectures and what you've learned from experiences. Learning from experience is so much deeper and longer-lasting because it comes with emotions like regret or pride. Those emotions help you own it. Stories evoking emotion are the next best thing to experience—they don't happen to us firsthand, but they can still touch our emotions and give us the glue that heightens our ability to understand, remember, and own the information.

Let's hear it from some brainiacs

Dr. Paul Zak and his colleagues at the Center for Neuro-economic Studies have conducted countless experiments on the stickiness of stories. As mentioned in Chapter 1, he and his colleagues have been able to correlate these to the levels of oxytocin, cortisol, and other chemicals naturally found in our bodies, which they monitor with brain and heart scans and blood analysis. So it's about as scientific and rigorous as it gets. Here's Dr. Zak on what they've found:

"From an impact perspective, when you have these human-scale stories that also embody emotion, they're much more memorable. They have much more impact in the moment, and later on down the road. We've done studies where we looked at recall and these deep character stories are recalled much better. Even if they don't relate to you directly."

Researchers M. Carolyn Clark and Marsha Rossiter found the same results in their work. In their research paper called "Narrative Learning in Adulthood," they wrote:

"Stories draw us into an experience at more than a cognitive level; they engage our spirit, our imagination, our heart, and this engagement is complex and holistic. Good stories transport us away from the present moment, sometimes even to another level of consciousness. They evoke other experiences we've had, and those experiences become real again."

Sounds like a drug, doesn't it? Well, what Clark and Rossiter described points to something else Dr. Zak and his team found that's even more powerful than stickiness. They found emotional stories also open people up to new ideas and prepare them for action. Here's Dr. Zak again:

"One reason that this emotional resonance can change our beliefs is because oxytocin is active in the areas of the brain that are associated with social memories. As social creatures, once we absorb the story, once we're transported into it and become part of it in a real way, then we're actually forming memories that tell us how to solve a problem or how some issue might be resolved."

Dr. Keith Oatley, Professor Emeritus of Cognitive Psychology at the University of Toronto, also saw this connection from story to emotion to openness to adoption. Here's what he says happens to us when we're touched by movies:

"At a film, we put aside our own goals and plans and insert goals and plans [of the characters]... into our own planning processor (the mental mechanism we use for making plans and carrying out actions in the world). Then, with the goals and plans we have taken on, we experience our own emotions in the circumstances that occur with the character's actions."

Dr. Oatley's not alone. We've all walked out of theaters feeling different. Movies bake emotion into their story strategy, and because of it, they're especially successful at influencing audiences. They bring us to spontaneously kiss our loved ones right after a romantic movie, feel tougher after seeing an action flick, even shape our political thoughts and opinions.

For instance, *An Inconvenient Truth* brought global warming to the mainstream discussion. *Blackfish* changed the way Sea World treats its whales. One of the most amazing shifts I personally saw in American culture happened right after the release of two movies: *Coming Home* and the 1978 best picture winner, *The Deer Hunter*. I'll speak here about *The Deer Hunter* because it's the one I remember being more affectual at the time. Before *The Deer Hunter*, you rarely saw vets honored publicly. Vietnam vets, especially, were often treated like lazy, whiny bums. But then came *The Deer Hunter*, a war movie 180° different from those John Wayne films where it seems like the enemy's guns have no bullets. *The Deer Hunter* told an emotional story, where audiences saw the soldiers in torturous conditions, felt their powerlessness and pain, and understood on a much deeper level why these soldiers were still spiraling after coming home. Audiences felt for them, and while I didn't have brain scans or heart monitors at the time, I witnessed a dramatic shift in our society. People thought differently about vets they saw on the street. They began to respect and honor them. It led to what we have today, where soldiers are heralded at sporting and civic events and given first entry onto airplanes. It's so ingrained in our current experience that it's hard to imagine anything different, but I swear I never saw that happen in the '70s before *The Deer Hunter*.

The Deer Hunter *helped change the way Americans viewed Vietnam War veterans.*

An Inconvenient Truth *did a fabulous job of using emotion to reinforce fact. The facts opened my eyes, but this animated polar bear is what made me cry, and then fume. Watch it at gettotheheartbook.com/movies*

"By eliciting emotions, watching movies can open doors that otherwise might stay closed."

- Dr. Birgit Wolz

Like I said, I'm not a scientist so I can only speculate, but Dr. Birgit Wolz is a psychologist and has also seen the power movies have to open the emotions that shape our perspective. She's a leading practitioner in the growing field of cinema therapy. Here's what she's found in her work:

> "Because many films transmit ideas through emotion rather than intellect, they can neutralize the instinct to suppress feelings and trigger emotional release. By eliciting emotions, watching movies can open doors that otherwise might stay closed."

The one-three punch

While emotion is supremely powerful, in a high-stakes business presentation where decisions might mean billions of dollars and the careers of many people, I think it's important and responsible to speak to the rational as well. Even though the elephant will move them, I want the driver onboard too, so we know their action is sound and headed for success. We can speak to both sides of the brain in an approach I call "the one-three punch." It's based on passion, understanding, and confidence.

For the rational side, we'll provide understanding in the same clear way we did in earlier chapters, so stakeholders can easily internalize it and relay it to others in the same credible and convincing way we did when we pitched it. I like to think of this as hitting them in the head.

And on the emotional side, we'll hit them in the heart and gut, unleashing their passion and instilling confidence in our information and ideas so they can help us see them through to success.

We've seen the one-three punch executed in those keynote, arena-filling presentations by elite speakers. They inform, but they also rally. As a result, everyone comes out raring to go. Steve Jobs was especially successful at it because Steve knew that passion is the only way (outside of desperation) to truly get stakeholders to innovate.

So here's how to get your Steve on, and how passion, understanding, and confidence can build off one another to bring you buy-in, action, and success.

Passion

The intoxicant that gets them to engage and emotionally attach. It comes from the empathy they feel for the characters you've presented in your story, the desire to help them, in the competitive spark to beat someone else, or the vision of themselves at their best. It's also what makes them want to share your ideas.

Understanding

The tools and intelligence to get the job done right. Knowledge of the dynamics of the situation and the players that shape it; the opportunities that spring from them and ways to capitalize on them. It's the tools you give your stakeholders so they don't look like idiots once they've shared your ideas, because you've ignited their passion.

Confidence

What enables them to own the ideas. It's what sustains the passion you've unleashed and makes the understanding you've given them taste like Kool-Aid to the other people they recruit, such as their bosses or teams. Understanding may keep them from looking like an idiot, but confidence will make sure they don't feel like one.

UNDERSTANDING

Head, Heart, Gut: The One-Three Punch that inspires buy-in

PASSION

CONFIDENCE

Where to start building your one-three punch

Just like any other message, the one-three punch starts with understanding your stakeholders. But because we are in Emotionland, I want you to go deeper and not just understand them—I want you to empathize with them, like the audiences who saw *The Deer Hunter*. I know that may seem hokey or feel like a lot of work (especially if you don't think your stakeholders deserve your empathy), but stick with me—as my wife will attest, I am not a naturally empathetic person, but I have seen its power. Empathy not only makes my work far more effective and my relationships stronger, but also makes my day a lot more fulfilling. It even makes annoying people more enjoyable. It's also the most dignified way to gain success in a corporation— far more respectable than brown-nosing or showboating.

Because aside from some serial killers, we are all emotional people, driven by our elephants, and empathy brings our elephants together. You understand me, I understand you. You become more open to me, I'll become more open to you, your ideas, and your solutions. I see that you've thought about me, so I want to give you the green light and enough budget.

But keep this in mind: while it has huge strategic benefits, you cannot approach empathy like a transaction. You really need to open yourself up to seeing your stakeholders as people, taking in their situations in a human way, and giving them a bit of your heart. Like I said, it may hurt at first, but in the end, you'll feel better about it because you'll feed your own elephant, feel a deeper purpose, and get more empathy in return.

Where did a heartless person like me learn all this? From the movies—watching heroes I cared about opening themselves up. I started with characters I felt akin to, but soon found myself feeling for characters across the spectrum. I still do it today. If I want to feel empathy for someone and it doesn't come naturally, I try to find a movie with a character similar to that person. It works with surprising regularity, and it's way cheaper than a shrink.

How movies move the elephant

This empathy-evoking effect that movies have is quite intentional. I'm sure playwrights and novelists do this as well, but in all great movies, there are two ways they get us to empathize. The first is by giving the hero a weakness. Screenwriters know that vulnerability will make us care about them. It's their road into our hearts, especially if it's something we can relate to in our non-hero lives. For instance, none of us are going to be chased by Nazis, so George Lucas, Lawrence Kasdan and Philip Kaufman also made Indiana Jones afraid of snakes. They knew that would bond us with Indy because it gave us something to relate to. Dorothy is just a little girl, no match physically or magically for the Wicked Witch, and we've all felt that. Harry Potter and Luke Skywalker both suffer from not knowing their parents. Our parental disconnect may be different, but this character device still brings us back to our longing, bonding us closer to those heroes by having us feel for them.

It even works when the hero is otherwise completely unlikable. None of us, for instance, would ever want to

None of us are going to be chased by Nazis, so the writers also made Indiana Jones afraid of snakes.

They knew that would bond us with Indy because it gave us something we could relate to.

hang out with Tony Soprano. He's a bully, a hothead, and a bit of a whiner. But because the screenwriter also gave him severe anxiety and relatives even worse than Tony, we can feel for the big goombah.

Character Arcs

The other way screenwriters craft empathy is by giving the hero two story arcs: an outer arc and an inner arc. You see and hear the outer arc onscreen in the hero's words and actions. It's the surface story that expresses what the hero wants: to win the game, get the girl, save the universe, etc.

The inner arc is based on what the hero truly needs. It expresses the theme of the movie. You also see and hear it onscreen, but it's usually more subtle, not the straightforward line that signifies the outer arc. It might be delivered in the way the actors says the words or the actions or reactions to them, rather than the words themselves. It might be a look in his/her eye. Either way, it's actually more powerful because it's the one where

our hero develops as a person worthy of what they want, or the one who has grown so much they no longer really need it, so it transcends the story and touches us personally.

In most movies, the hero starts on the outer arc and ends up on the inner. Oftentimes that's because the two arcs come together, like *The Wizard of Oz*, where Dorothy wants to go home, but needs to appreciate it and feel appreciated. She gets both, and because we see her develop from a bratty teen to the savior of Oz, we also feel like she deserves to get both. Yay Dorothy!

In many great movies, though, the hero starts on the outer arc, but then gets pulled away to the inner arc, eventually transcending their outer arc. We do as well when we watch the movie because we subconsciously take up their cause. For instance, in *Casablanca*, Rick's outer arc—what he wants—is to reunite with Ilsa. His inner arc, though, is based on what he truly needs: to reunite with his moral sense of purpose.

Movies and marketing are both based on two premises: the thing we want, and the thing we need.

We see Rick's inner arc beginning to hold sway at the story's turning point, one of the three key scenes we'll talk about in Chapter 5. It's intentional and meant to signal to us that Rick is buying into the theme of the movie. It comes when, even though his café is full of Nazis, Rick allows the band to play "La Marseillaise." It's a huge moment that makes us scared for Rick. But because we also see that his jaded veneer is starting to crack, it takes our relationship with Rick to a deeper level. We can see he's growing and becoming the hero we know he needs to be. And then, at the end, when he tells Ilsa to board the plane with Victor, we know his heart is transformed. So even though he doesn't have Ilsa (the thing he wanted), we know he now has something far more important—his moral purpose—so we feel even more fulfilled than if he had just gotten Ilsa. Yay Rick!

Marketing takes a cue
Modern marketing is also based on these two premises. There's the product, and there's the emotional benefit we give our target. The rational would suggest building the brand around the product features like they did back in the 1950s-pitchman days ("It slices, it dices!" etc.). But today, great marketers know that an emotional benefit will touch people more deeply. They want the target to identify with the brand, not just the features, so they start their process with our good friend empathy. Harley-Davidson is a perfect example. The real sell for Harley is empathizing with the people who feel caged and demoralized by the status quo, so they offer them dignity, freedom, and a

community of rebels they can join. For their target, it's been a wonderful thing. Harley riders can easily buy a faster, more reliable, and cheaper bike, but Harley strikes that emotional chord for them so no other motorcycle will do.

Similarly, the idea behind this book is not a desire to share what I learned in film class; there are far better books for that. It came from two places: from all the presentations I've attended that bored me so much I wanted to off myself, and from the work I did creating insights and strategy deliverables at Cheskin. Every day I was there, I collaborated with brilliant people who worked their butts off, poured their hearts into their projects, and developed gold for our clients. But that didn't ensure that insights and ideas would be adopted, not by a long shot. There were many successes, but also a lot of phenomenal work that ended up in some filing cabinet (a place one of my clients calls "the morgue"). Seeing that happen too many times absolutely broke my heart.

So that's what I'm trying to do with this book: right that wrong. As I mentioned in Chapter 1, I know the problem is widespread and a lot of you probably have brilliant ideas sitting in the morgue as well. My inner arc is that need for your ideas to get heard so you can make a bigger difference. That would give me such a warm feeling and absolutely make my day. So if you experience success through anything you learn in this book, please write me at ted@gettotheheartbook.com.

Most execs and directors are in meetings all day. Each one the same: dull conference room, charts on a screen. Take a minute to imagine being one of them.

Back to empathy

Your stakeholders also have their outer and inner arcs. In Chapter 2, when we talked about considering our stakeholders' plan for your information, we extended our reach into that inner arc. But we can take it further now by spending a little time thinking about their emotional situation, like Harley-Davidson does for its riders. Don't worry, I'm not talking forever, just until we develop our relationship with them so they can open up to us.

In Chapter 1, I mentioned Paul Magnone and Christopher Frank's book *Drinking from the Fire Hose* because a vivid depiction of an executive's emotional situation will help us empathize.

Here are some exceprts where Paul and Chris describe a typical meeting from a stakeholder's point of view:

> "The presenter finally makes it to slide four…At least you can read this one, unlike the first three, which were so crammed with numbers, graphs, and charts…you couldn't figure out what they meant...
>
> You look around the room, wondering whether anyone else is actually following the presentation…
>
> Another slide appears. You can't tell why. The presenter reads every word and every number….
>
> Finally, someone calls for a 'time check,' …
>
> You…scramble to identify as many action items as you can in a vain attempt to show that the meeting had some purpose."

Sound familiar? I wouldn't be surprised if this describes an experience you had today. Even if you've never had to sit through a meeting like this, does reading this allow you to see execs in a different light? If you feel for them, congrats; you're already empathizing!

Now imagine if your presentation wasn't like everyone else's that day, and you gave them something completely different. Something refreshing and meaningful that hit them with that one-three punch. You'd be the highlight of their day. They would think you're amazing and they'd even listen.

The empathizing wake-up call

I lead storytelling workshops where we storify a real presentation the department needs to give. In it, we do breakout sessions and one group gets the responsibility of creating the presentation's opening. We pay a lot of attention to it because it's where stakeholders will decide if you are worth listening to. So I instruct them to start by—yeah, I'm going to say it again—empathizing. I ask them questions about their stakeholders because I know it will lead them to empathy, a deeper understanding, and the ability to hook their stakeholders in a meaningful way. Here's what I ask:

- What are their jobs really about?
- What are they judged on when they have to report to their bosses?
- What kind of pressure are they under right now?

One group I worked with had an expensive initiative they were going to pitch to the C-suite. They felt their chances were good because they knew their initiative fit in with the vision of the company.

But then their company got acquired, so a whole new set of execs were flying in. That made it about a billion times tougher. Now it wasn't just about how much the initiative would cost; it was that cost, on top of the $2 billion investment the new company had already made to acquire their company.

Still, they ran through these questions and took time to imagine what those execs from New York were going through. Soon their empathy began to flow:

<u>What are their jobs really about?</u>
These execs' jobs are all about setting up their new acquisition for success, so they can get back the $2 billion their bosses just spent.

<u>What are they judged on when they have to report to their bosses?</u>
They are judged on the ROI they reap from this new company they barely know, and may not have bought themselves if they were in charge. So it's not only a difficult task, it's also really scary because they don't have the same amount of control they would have over people they hired themselves.

<u>What kind of pressure are they under right now?</u>
Their own company is known for having a fiercely competitive culture, and their CEO is famous for turning companies around. This one must also succeed.

The effect was pretty amazing. Because the group thought about the execs' emotional dynamic, they were able to see them not as conquering titans coming in to lay down edicts, but as people under a ton of pressure that really need to go back to New York with good news. My group then realized that their initiative could be some of that good news, so they decided to position it in that direction and highlight the initiative's upside as a counterpoint to the massive investment the acquiring company just made. A story of acknowledgement leading to empathy leading to solution.

So this group's idea for opening the presentation was designed specifically to do that, but also to wake up the execs in a meaningful way. It included two powerful attention-spiking devices you see all the time in movies and magic: motion and suspense. When the execs walked in, the first thing they would see is two big TVs. One would show the words "$2 billion" in big white letters on a black screen so it could be easily read from anywhere in the room. The second TV would show another large number, but this one would be constantly rising—like a ticker—in super-fast motion. The rising number would be a growing tally of the revenue that their proposed opportunity would generate if the company decided to move forward.

Imagine: after an interminable day of four boring PowerPoint presentations in a row, you walk in to see that big upticking TV. Could you take your eyes off it? I couldn't. But before I could even commend the group's idea, they told me about the second plan they had for the upticking TV. It was equally brilliant. After explaining the screen to the execs, they would put a cloth over it—with the promise of unveiling the new number at the end of the presentation so the execs could see how much revenue grew in just the 45 minutes they'd been sitting there. Talk about suspense. Talk about movie-style storytelling.

Of course, whenever you do something bold like that, you have to back it up. Being dataheads, they did have realistic and vetted projections. But instead of showing a static slide that says "$100 million market" and having it go in one ear and out the other, they went bold. They went visual. They evoked emotion in a group that was surely tired, stressed, and in need of a visceral experience to cut through the jet lag. They also gave their stakeholders more: a story they could tell when they got back to headquarters and reported on the outlook of the new acquisition. That presentation showed smarts and moxie, and absolutely delivered the one-three punch: understanding, passion, and confidence. And it all started with taking a little bit of time to empathize.

A practical way to empathize
Most people tailor the length of their presentations to the stakeholders they're presenting to, but mostly

This group's idea for opening the presentation was designed to wake up the execs in a meaningful way.

It included two powerful attention-spiking devices you see all the time in movies and magic:

Motion and suspense.

because they're told in advance that they have only x number of minutes to present. But let me show you how you can go further and tailor the <u>style</u> of your presentation to your stakeholders and really maximize your ability to empathize and get a seat at the table.

Everyone has a natural way they learn. I'm sure you do. Yours might be visual, or musical, or experiential. Whatever it is, your preference makes the process of learning easier and more enjoyable. It also makes it stick. Figuring out the easiest path for your stakeholders to learn and retain your information will give them those same benefits. It will also help you determine the way you should tell your story.

Here's how it's done: you know how companies segment their customers? A car manufacturer, for instance, develops a truck for one type of customer and a minivan for another? Their ad agencies also create different messages for each segment so their ads are more meaningful. Those segments are usually laid out on a grid, mapped by the attitudes and priorities that shape each segment's decisions and actions. They call it a segmentation model.

So we're going to take a page out of their playbook, but we're going to flip it. Instead of segmenting customers, we're going to segment employees, and in particular, the people you present to.

Of course, everyone is different, and your approach should be tailored to the person rather than the po-

sition, but generally speaking, I've found stakeholders tend to differ by:

- Level of detail they want

- Whether they like their information in a practical or emotional form

To the right, you'll see our stakeholder segmentation model.

Let's plot some job titles, starting with execs. We all know execs like their information short and sweet, but why? Well, if we take a moment to picture their day and empathize, it not only becomes more clear, but provides a deeper insight. Execs have to sit in meetings, take in information, and make decisions, all under immense pressure. When you're in that situation, what do you want most? You want that person to get to the point, right? "Cut to the chase," as they say in Hollywood. Because when you're under pressure, so much of your energy goes into trying to filter out the extra words, and it's hard not to go numb. Next time you have to prepare something for execs, go back to that feeling. You'll soon be right in their shoes and completely understand the beauty of "short and sweet."

But now, let's go deeper. The second big part of an exec's job is to lead people. So even more effective than being "short and sweet" is being memorable and evoking confidence. A compact, memorable package, with phrases and images an exec can take "to go," makes

Stakeholder Segmentation Model

EMOTIONAL

Ad agencies

Marketing

Executives

Designers

COMPREHENSIVE

PITHY

Researchers

Developers and engineers

Strategists

PRACTICAL

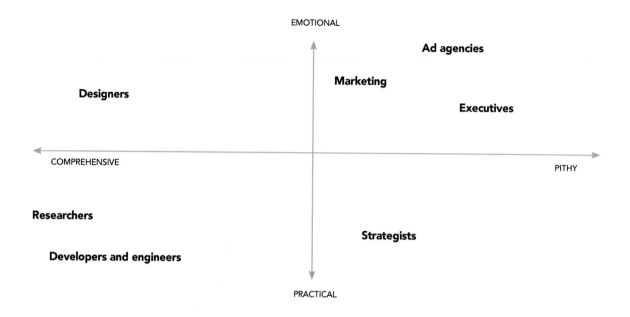

EMOTIONAL

Ad agencies

Marketing

Designers

Executives

COMPREHENSIVE

PITHY

Researchers

Strategists

Developers and engineers

PRACTICAL

it so much easier for them to go back to their departments and inspire their teams around your ideas. That's why execs like stories, because stories are memorable, sharable packages. A two-minute movie (yes, I'm plugging my favorite medium again) is the perfect package for presenting your message to an exec: a short, sweet, sharable story that tells itself.

Now let's move diagonally to the lower-left square of the model. Here you'll find researchers and engineers who want detail, and lots of it. I've found that they develop confidence and trust when they can spend time with the information and develop their own story with it. A war room, with all the facts pinned to the walls, is a perfect way to do that. They should also be taken through the information in an easy-to-follow story

so you know they get it, but then, let them spend a week with the information to build up that trust.

Moving up to the top-left square, industrial and interface designers also like a lot of detail and will appreciate a war room. But because designers require the important feedback of customers as they experience a product, they prefer to see and hear those consumers instead of just reading about them (again, perfect place for a movie). They also like their information visual, tactile, and experiential, so bringing in pictures and products—even from completely different business categories—really works for them.

Now let's move to the right. Ad agencies and marketing people like everything to be simple: get it down to thirty seconds. But in the world of advertising, it also needs emotional resonance; after all, brands are all about emotions.

Finally, moving down to the bottom, I've never seen a strategist let anyone go ten minutes in a presentation without hijacking it. So for them, I suggest tools and games so they can get their hands dirty. Games also work for salespeople, feeding into their competitive natures, especially those games that allow them to embarrass their co-workers. (Actually, who am I kidding—embarrassing co-workers works for everybody.)

Take a minute and plot yourself on the model. See what feels natural to you. Now try plotting your spouse or significant other. If you consider their natural learning style every time you pitch to them, it might get you out of one of those boring dinners they drag you to.

Then, before you start your next presentation, plot your stakeholders on this model and see if it changes the length and form you want to take with your presentation. Maybe you'll find PowerPoint slides aren't the only option. Maybe it will give you a whole new avenue to make your presentation easier on them, and also easier on you.

I've found the war room did that because I didn't have to prepare a summary or conclusions for everything. Same thing when I did 2-minute videos for marketing, instead of the 10-minute versions I used to do. What a time saver that's been. Yay empathy!

THE BIG TAKEAWAYS
from this chapter

5

Even in the business world, we are all motivated more by emotion than rational thought.

Evoking emotion and empathy releases oxytocin and cortisol and can even fire neurons that open us up to new ideas.

Movies intentionally craft their stories and heroes to evoke empathy by constructing weaknesses we can relate to and by giving them an inner arc we ride on vicariously. This is why movies like *The Deer Hunter* can accomplish what few other communication platforms can: change minds.

Empathizing with your stakeholders on an emotional level will not only open you up to new ideas, but it makes it easier for them to buy into yours.

By flipping the traditional customer segmentation model, you can craft your presentation method to work with your stakeholders' natural learning styles and come away with greater results.

New Case in Point:

Breakthrough medical device for diabetes

Like our Capital One example, this case history is inspired by actual projects we've done, but because we can't disclose details of our work, it's made up. It does outline the approach we would most likely come in with. But here's one of the most fun things about strategic storytelling: by the time I got to hear more about the corporate culture and collaborate with the clients, we would probably end up with something even more inspiring and effective.

Anyway, today we're out of finance and deep into the fast-rising world of medical devices. Everyone sees huge potential in this category, so it's captured not only the interest of health companies, but also tech entrepreneurs, and the venture capitalists who can fund them.

Tech entrepreneurs know the established companies in this category have the advantage of experience and a network of doctors and distributors, but they also know that between innovative thought, slick design, and even slicker technology, they can develop a product that can quickly gain attention, desire, and market share. The Nest Learning Thermostat is a perfect example. I can only imagine what the environment has been like at Honeywell since the Nest came out.

On the other hand, the established companies in biotech see the startups coming and know they must innovate to protect their market share. But everyone needs targeted inspiration, and that comes from two things: truly understanding the needs of patients and the desire to transform that knowledge into a breakthrough product and business model. In other words, they need both sides of their brains fed to get that understanding and passion. And since developing a medical device is a multimillion-dollar investment, they also need confidence to keep pouring money in through all the development, testing, and government compliance protocols. In other words, the stakes are high. Sounds like a perfect case for us to review and apply everything we learned about emotion, right? So let's do it.

Since our last case history involved us working with the relatively newer bank Capital One, how about this time we go to work for the firmly established Johnson & Johnson? They have a division called LifeScan which is currently the second largest manufacturer of blood glucose monitors.

Glucose monitors tell diabetics if they need insulin. You prick your finger, put some blood on a test strip, and insert it into the device to find out. Then, if you need insulin, you give yourself a shot.

There is also a device called an insulin pump, which, through a needle already inserted into the patient, delivers insulin all day long. While still not accurate enough to be completely automatic, the popularity of insulin pumps has grown, and LifeScan has taken notice.

But what if LifeScan took it a step further and fused the two products, developing a device smart enough to monitor insulin levels on its own and deliver the appropriate amount to keep the patient steady and healthy? That would be huge.

Well, now we know our job: use the power of emotion to enable and inspire LifeScan to develop this breakthrough product.

First order of business: empathy
As mentioned, one of LifeScan's key traits is that it is established. It has established products, methods, and departmental roles. Theoretically, that should make it far less nimble and slower than a Silicon Valley startup. This theory has not escaped the teams at LifeScan. It's both a sore spot and an actual fear.

But the truth is that it's also only one theory. Here's another: if a company is larger, with more people and resources, and if all those people and resources are working together with synergy and zeal, shouldn't that actually make it faster and more nimble than a startup, like a hockey team at full strength?

So that was the attitude we went with, and the credit and challenge we wanted to instill within the LifeScan:

They think we're the
Titanic, but they're wrong.

We have more specialized
talent, more resources, and
more experience. On what
planet is that a bad thing?
Guess it's time to give
the world a little reality check.

Oh, and one other thing:
We're not just here for an IPO.
We're here to help people.

It was pure emotion, designed to strike two chords: "We have a true purpose," and "We have something to prove." Both fit the sentiment of the people at LifeScan and both are highly motivating.

Next we looked at the various stakeholders we needed to present to.

Executives:
Everyone knows that getting buy-in at the C-level ensures buy-in everywhere else, so getting them to fire people up goes a long way.

Execs need an overall understanding of where the opportunities are, and how they're going to be leveraged by each of the individual departments. They also need key messages to lead their teams. But because their time is precious, they need all that in a compact, cut-to-the-chase kind of package.

Product Development:
Made up of scientists, researchers, designers, and engineers, these are the people that need the whole truth and appreciate a lot of detail. They have the patience to figure it out on their own, but with the clock ticking, it doesn't hurt to also give them a guided tour.

To create a breakthrough product, they need to deeply understand the relationship between patients and their devices. When and how the devices are used, when they're not, and how patients hack them into submission to make them more useful. They need to know the pain points of the current products and the effect that pain has on patients. And through all that, they need to stay inspired.

Marketing:
Though medical devices are becoming consumer products, there's still a lot of attention that needs to be paid to the influence of the doctor and his/her role in keeping the patient on protocol; helping to foster the relationship between doctors and patients is key.

And devices aren't cheap, so marketing also has to be cognizant of the financial picture and mindful of the insurance companies that often pay for the devices.

Throughout, though, marketing managers need to focus on the emotional journey of the patient, mitigating fears and keeping patients feeling as empowered as possible.

So because each of these stakeholders is tackling the mission from a different angle, they each have very different needs.

You know I never like to make these case histories easy.

And even with these very different groups of stakeholders, we still need to make sure our presentation

> When the "something to prove" mantra feels like it's wearing thin, we'll replace it with something even more inspiring: a poster-child hero who provides a common language.

accomplished three big feats: deliver the information that will inspire innovation, enable synergy between the departments, and motivate everyone to challenge established practices and come up with ideas that are new, bold, and right.

Pony-up time
How will we do that? We'll use the one-three punch and pack it with emotion:

Passion:
We'll start with the "something to prove" mantra from a couple pages back so it rallies everyone together in a unified sense of purpose. When it feels like it's starting to wear thin, we'll replace it with something even more inspiring: a hero that can provide everyone a common language. A very real patient that everyone can innovate around. So it won't be a faceless population called "diabetics." It will be one diabetic, with a name, a face, and an archetypal

experience. That will make innovating much more manageable, and the ability to synergize much easier.

We'll also work with corporate communications to spread this hero's story—and our mission to help him or her—to the entire company, so the teams can be encouraged outside their buildings as well, and will know the whole company is pulling for them—and yes, feel that extra bit of pressure that comes with that spotlight.

Understanding:
Having one central hero will also make it easier for everyone to understand. While still representing the whole, it won't be abstract data anymore, but one person's experience. That will allow us to go deeper with the information and hit them at that gut and heart level, as well as in the head, so it really sinks in.

At the same time, because these groups are so different, we'll make three separate presentations so each group will hear what they need to hear, and not hear what they don't. That simplicity will make it far easier for them to stay energized and focused.

Confidence:
On the exec level, we'll share our multi-pronged campaign so they'll know that everyone's getting the goods they need, but in a way that brings them together. We'll also keep them apprised of progress and try to get the execs to send encouraging messages to the teams, based on their actual progress, rather than just the typical blanket slogans.

Those messages will go far on the departmental level, but we'll also keep everyone further inspired and confident by holding departmental show-and-tells where they can keep one another inspired.

Our Hero
LifeScan employees are used to seeing patients in their 50s and older with type-2 diabetes (the kind that onsets later and is often attributed to extra weight). They represent a huge portion of patients and are the most common focus group attendees. But because employees have already heard so many of their stories, we think they may have grown numb to them. We need the teams to approach this project with a fresh perspective, so it would help if our hero was someone different than who they're used to seeing.

Yes, our hero needs to be archetypal, with implications common enough to apply to the entire market, but he or she can still be different enough to shake the status quo, challenge assumptions, and get everyone to take that fresh look necessary for innovation.

LifeScan has a large CRM database, filled with patients and data about their condition, history, and protocol (medical-speak for treatment plan). Many of these patients have corresponded directly with LifeScan to provide product feedback. We'll start there and also enlist a market research recruiter to find patients who use insulin pumps.

Through the recruiter, we find an insulin-pump user named Taylor. She's perfect.

Taylor is not the typical over-50 type-2 diabetic that LifeScan had grown used to seeing. She's 22, fit, and enjoys a good time. She's fresh out of college, where she was in a sorority and loved every minute of it. Now she's just graduated and she's as full of desire and dreams as anyone her age.

Feeling compassion for her yet? That's exactly what we're counting on and why we decide to open Taylor's story with her talking about how awesome college was. In our video, we even show her running, then in a bar, enjoying cocktails and having a great time with her friends.

Why?

Four reasons:

1. That will help make Taylor different enough to shake up assumptions and put LifeScan employees in a different frame of mind. Again, that's key when you want to innovate like a startup. Taylor helps us check that box perfectly.

2. Remember how heroes can be even more inspiring when they're relatable? When we looked around the LifeScan offices, we didn't find many diabetics over 50 working there. The teams we want to inspire have far more in common with Taylor than the patients they're used to seeing. Many are even close enough to Taylor's age to identify with that expansive, dream-filled time of life. Others have children Taylor's age and vicariously carry those desires.

3. Focusing on a younger person will also force designers to keep their solutions portable, which we know will be a key factor for the success of the product, and will force marketing people to think about the long term as well as today.

4. The stories LifeScan employees see or hear about patients are usually set on a level emotional plane. Here's patient A, here's how she manages her diabetes, and how she struggles. They're all heartening, but the emotional level is constant.

   On the other hand, by first showing Taylor as a happy-go-lucky young person, we can start everyone off on a higher emotional plane. They see her at the bar with her friends, they hear how much she loves her life, they settle into her story and have a defined sense of her. And then, all of a sudden, when we reveal that she's a diabetic whose life is far from

When we all experience the same emotional fall, it creates a unifying moment that sets everyone up to become emotionally invested in Taylor and her story.

In movies they call this "the inciting incident."

easy, everyone feels the same emotional fall. That creates a unifying moment that sets everyone up for emotional investment in Taylor and her story. In movie terms, they call this "the inciting incident." It's the first of the three key scenes and sets the story in motion. We meet the hero going through his or her life, then comes the inciting incident and they have no choice but to act. In *Star Wars*, the inciting incident is when Luke sees Leia in the hologram. In *Casablanca*, it's when Ilsa shows up. In *The Wizard of Oz*, it's the tornado plopping Dorothy in Munchkinland. This emotional fall, we thought, could be LifeScan's inciting incident. By dropping the emotional plane so everyone feels Taylor's plight, we set up a huge gap between what should be and what is. This gap will define the mission to solve the problems diabetics experience and get both Taylor and us back up to the original emotional plane.

Is this kind of emotional manipulation wrong? When I talk about it in these terms, it may seem at least creepy. But think of the good that can come from it. A team galvanized and working together toward a pursuit that is actually noble, an innovative product created, a heritage company employing thousands of people strengthened, and millions of people suffering from a disease given a better way of life. Sounds good to me.

Custom-tailored movies

Because they're such fantastic vehicles for showing patient experiences and emotion, we decide to anchor our campaign with videos. Videos are also modular, like PowerPoint slides, so they enable us to develop different versions for each of our different stakeholders. Each video will show different aspects of Taylor and her experience so we can be as relevant and inspiring as possible. They'll also feature title cards that highlight opportunities to help Taylor. The product development version will show more interaction with the device and highlight opportunities to make it more functional and fit more easily into Taylor's life. It will also be the longest version. The marketing version will focus on the emotional experience, the doctor relationship, and Taylor's financial fears, and then show opportunities where marketing might be able to relieve her anxiety and empower her. The executive version will be a summary showing both sets of opportunities so the execs can know what's being worked on. Finally, the company version will be stripped down, but still emotional, to give J&J employees a way to keep everyone inspired.

All the movies will open with the same setup and emotional drop I discussed earlier, and end with the modest but meaningful goal Taylor shares: to be free and spontaneous enough to just run off to Mexico.

For each stakeholder, we will play their version of the movie, then spend the rest of an afternoon ideating (the corporate word for "brainstorming") on the various opportunities highlighted. As you'll see when you watch them, these opportunities are around a specific problem Taylor describes. That provides the context to make the teams feel it and enables them to focus. For that moment, they don't have to solve a global problem affecting a huge population. All they have to do is help Taylor with that one issue, then later scale their ideas so they have global applicability. That will be a billion times easier.

We'll also give each of the teams different sets of stimuli. For the designers and engineers, we'll fill the conference room with dozens of photos of Taylor's experience and belongings and give them ample time to take them in. We'll also give each team member a journal Taylor completed, detailing her day-to-day activities, her interaction with her device and medicine, and her feelings at each moment.

The marketing department will also hear about the experiences and feelings Taylor described (along with those of other patients we superimposed into Taylor's journals), but for them, we'll make the stories more brief and visual on large posters so they can really feel the emotion that speaks to their natural learning style.

To the right are the development and marketing versions of the movies with Taylor so you can see how emotion can heighten understanding and inspire people in a way that speaking only to the rational just can't match.

Play the product-development version
You'll find it at gettotheheartbook.com/movies

Play the marketing version
You'll find it at gettotheheartbook.com/movies

CHAPTER 5

Make It Move

by mapping it out in a truly sophisticated way

The storyline most often given in the upper echelon of business presentations isn't all that different from the classic high-school essay. We just graduated from sentences to bullet points. In Corporateland, it goes like this:

1. Tell them what you're going to tell them.

2. Tell them.

3. Tell them what you just told them.

Sounds perfectly fine, right? Simple to execute, with a nice logical flow?

Now put your empathy hat on, and imagine having to sit through six of those each day. How tedious would that be? In this chapter, we're going to get a lot more sophisticated.

We're going to discard "tell them what you're going to tell them," we're going to expand "tell them" to four more sophisticated steps, and we're going to fine-tune "tell them what you just told them" so it's less by-the-numbers and far more inspiring.

We're going to marry the rational with the emotional and get that one-three punch we talked about in the last chapter, and we'll map it out so we can go from the moment your stakeholders walk into the conference room all the way to a rallying cry that will make them want to get off their butts and make it happen.

The efficiency of mapping

Major motion pictures are always mapped out. Mapping helps screenwriters keep track of the story and plot out their scenes before they begin writing dialogue. It also makes the screenwriter's job easier and more efficient because they nearly always start with one of five established structures.

There's the Explosion structure, which guides nearly every disaster movie; there's the Branch structure, which enables us to watch three completely different storylines in a sitcom without getting confused; the Spiral structure, which you see in many thrillers like *Memento*; the Meandering structure in journey movies like *The Adventures of Huckleberry Finn*; and the most common of all, the one that screenwriters have been milking over and over again for thousands of years: Aristotle's Three Act Structure. Yep, that Aristotle, as in Greece, 335 BCE. Believe it or not, hundreds of your favorite movies

and thousands more are all based on a story structure developed by a guy in a toga (I know, it was a tunic, but "toga" sounds more Blutarsky). Why? Because it works. Is it formulaic? Absolutely. In fact, many screenwriting teachers can break the formula down by the minute. But when we sit in our seats and see it onscreen, do we care? If box office receipts are any indication, then the answer is an emphatic "no." Because even though we've seen the three-act structure a thousand times, it must jibe with our natural ability to absorb information and appreciate it. What a genius that Aristotle was. What a toga-wearing genius.

I've mentioned *Star Wars* a lot. It's a perfect example of the three-act structure. Check out the diagram to the right. The three key acts are the setup, the confrontation, and the resolution. In this diagram, they look equal in length, but it all depends on the pace of the movie. Often, especially in an action movie where the pace needs to quicken as the movie runs, act three is far shorter than the other acts.

Then there are three key scenes. The first is the inciting incident I wrote about in the last chapter. Again, this is where the story really kicks off. Before the inciting incident, the hero is going through his/her life in an everyday way, usually discontented. In the first act of *Star Wars*, Luke is whiling away on his aunt and uncle's farm. Then his inciting incident comes in the hologram message from Princess Leia. After that, his quest begins and, lo and behold, our discontented farm-boy is on his way to becoming a princess-saving badass.

The next key scene is the turning point I wrote about with Rick in *Casablanca*. It's usually right before the end of act two, but doesn't necessarily have to be. It's there to give the audience the emotional boost they'll need for act three by signaling to us that the hero finally understands the main lesson necessary to fulfill his/her destiny. In *Star Wars*, it's when Luke is in his X-wing fighter and hears Obi-Wan's voice speaking to him. It's a tense moment, but then we see him close his eyes and use the Force to launch the torpedo and we know he's a Jedi. Luke's relationship with the Force will define him far more than just saving the princess.

The final key scene is, of course, the climax, when the Death Star blows up. Spectacular, isn't it? Climaxes usually are.

Now check out that green line. It's called the dramatic arc. You see how it keeps climbing toward the climax, then quickly drops? It represents the level of tension and drama in the story. This green dramatic arc is the magic that glues us to our seats and makes us put movie posters on our walls. It's what makes us love movies. It's the push, push, push to the climax, then back down again, nice and easy, mostly so we can make it out of the theater without our pacemakers exploding.

It comes down to moments
My screenwriter friend Kevin Marburger told me something I'll never forget: "Movies are not about dialogue. They're about moments." If we were to zoom into that green line, moments are what we would see because

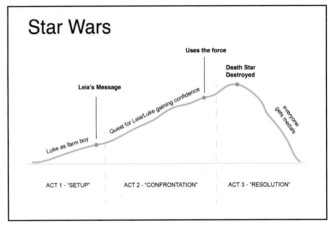

Star Wars is a perfect example of Aristotle's Three-Act Structure

> **"Movies are not about dialogue. They're about moments."**
>
> *- Screenwriter Kevin Marburger*

> **I agree, Kevin, and I even see it extending to life as a whole. It's all about moments.**
>
> *- Kevin's friend Ted Frank*

they're what drives it up and down. In both movies and real life, moments are what really move us and fill our memory banks. That's why directors and screenwriters make such an effort to create them, and why they plot them out in their maps.

When I learned that, I began to really study movies and look for the moments and what makes them so moving. Kevin was right. It isn't the dialogue as much as the tone the dialogue is delivered in, or the visuals and action that accompany it. That opened up so much for me, and not only because it freed me from having to write the perfect words every time. It showed me that *how* we hear the words is most important, not the words we hear. A perfect example is a romantic scene: the way a couple touches or looks at one another affects you infinitely more than their dialogue. In that moment, they could say something completely hokey and we'd still tear up. On the opposite end, remember when Lester throws the plate in *American Beauty*? Do you remember the dialogue? I don't, and I've seen that movie five times. But that plate smashing on the wall, and the release of pent-up hostility it represents—that's a moment I'll never forget.

I've found the power and magic of moments applies in real life as well. And in your presentations. You don't have to use the perfect words. If you can plot out some key moments, you too can raise and lower the green line and increase your resonance. In the last chapter, you read about how we did that with our movie for LifeScan. We'll talk in-depth about how to do it with your delivery in Chapter 11.

The dramatic arc gets measured

To test the power of the dramatic arc and the power of moments, Dr. Paul Zak and his team compared two different ways to deliver the same message—one with a dramatic arc and one without. He compared their viewers' blood samples, before and after watching the videos. He found that the video with the dramatic arc released cortisol and oxytocin in his subjects; the video without a story arc did not. Since cortisol focuses our attention and oxytocin makes us more empathic, caring, and connected, which video do you think was more powerful and persuasive?

A map for strategic presentations

When we develop a strategic story at Backstories Studio, we also have a story map where we plot out moments and create dramatic arcs, but because we designed ours specifically for corporate initiatives, it's a little different from the three-act structure and looks more like a strategic model. It's based on everything I've learned in the hundreds of strategic stories I've developed over the years. It doesn't apply to all strategic initiatives, but it works really well for most, and it's a perfect place for us to plot our journey together over the next few chapters.

The video with the dramatic arc released cortisol and oxytocin in the study's subjects; the video without a dramatic arc did not.

Since cortisol focuses our attention and oxytocin makes us more empathic, caring, and connected, which video do you think was more powerful and persuasive?

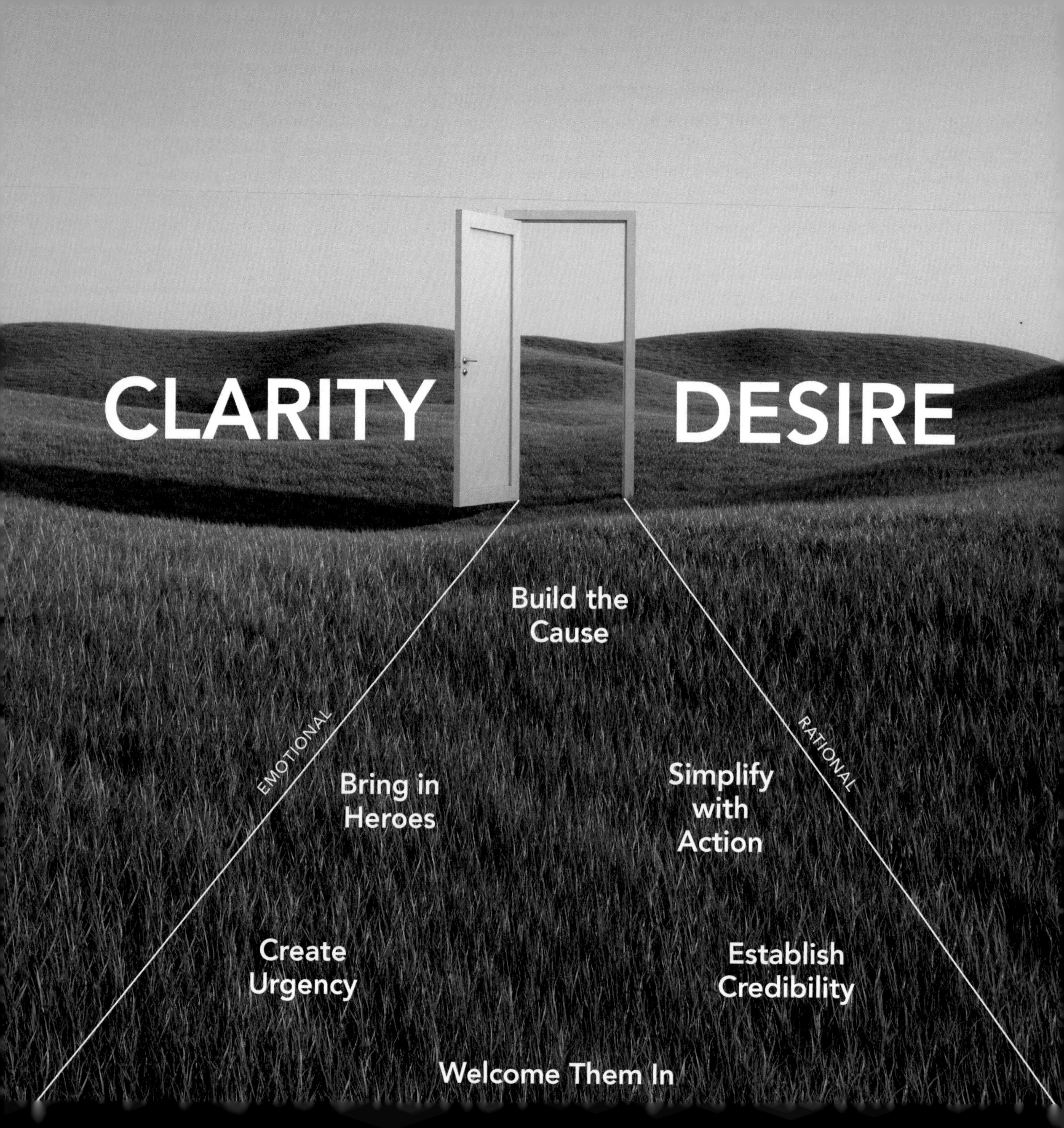

CLARITY

DESIRE

EMOTIONAL

RATIONAL

Build the
Cause

Bring in
Heroes

Simplify
with
Action

Create
Urgency

Establish
Credibility

Welcome Them In

You'll see this strategic story map on the left. It will guide the flow of the story so it's easy to follow. But because it also employs emotion, it will enable you to do so much more. See those two words on either side of the door: "Clarity" and "Desire"? If you've been applying what you learned in the previous chapters, you're probably getting pretty darn good at the clarity part. Now, young Padawan, you're going to up your game and apply the emotional cues you learned about in Chapter 4 and spark your stakeholders' desire. That is what will really get you those sexy high-ticket projects.

But Ted, where do I start?

Like many great movies, let's start at the end, with that door you see at the top of the map. That door represents what your stakeholders need to do. It's the answer to Big2 question #1: what do my stakeholders need to do? That might be repositioning the brand, creating a new product, persuading customers or investors, inspiring employees around a vision, or even just greenlighting your initiative. That door is the point at which your stakeholders enter the story to fulfill their destiny as the hero.

Our job as storytellers is to lead them to that door. To get them there, we're going to speak to both the elephant and the rider with those two rails that define the path.

The rational rail

Because this is business, we must have facts and statistics to feed the rational side. After all, these might be billion-dollar decisions, and you never want to shirk your responsibility of ensuring success. No flops. No blowback. No regrets. That doesn't mean you need to do it with text and figures, though. Action is a big part of feeding the rational, as you'll see in chapter nine.

The emotional rail

I know I've carried on quite a bit about the importance of emotion, so I'll spare you here. Just remember that the emotional rail is how you develop your stakeholders' desire. It also helps clear the haze in your stakeholders' eyes caused by the firehosing clowns they met with before they arrived at your presentation.

The path to the door

Using the rational and emotional rails, we're going to walk our stakeholders to the door. Each of these steps will get its own chapter, but here's a brief introduction to each:

1. Welcome them in
   This is where you seize their attention and get them out of the conference room and their phones and into your story, like my workshop group's upticking screen I wrote about earlier.

2. Create urgency
   Shows them what you're saying is not just important; it's important *right now*. They have to care and act. Time is of the essence.

In Corporateland, most people just aim for clarity. But desire is what really moves stakeholders, and yet almost no one goes there. Talk about opportunity.

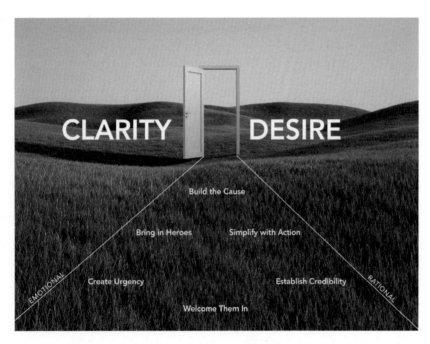

I know this photo is on a previous page, but in case you're lazy like me, I put in here for easy access.

3. <u>Establish credibility</u>
Shows them you're not full of it and builds the confidence that gives them permission to tell other people to listen to you.

4. <u>Bring in the heroes</u>
Attaches your information to a character (or real person) they can relate to, root for, and want to help. This will make them grasp your insights and ideas, remember them, and care.

5. <u>Simplify with action</u>
Shows them your information (instead of just telling them), which makes it much easier for them to understand.

It also makes them feel it (yeah, I know that's emotion, but the two rails are beginning to converge at this point). Also because it's either

visual or described vividly enough to visualize, seeing the action puts everyone on the
same page.

6. <u>Build the cause with confidence</u>
Wraps up your information into a cohesive,
actionable package they can use to spread
your revolution.

Here, confidence is evoked again so that
once they're through the door and on their
own, their passion can sustain. Things already
pointing in that direction have a great effect,
such as partnerships or assets that can be
leveraged, or initiatives already underway that
align with the goals of your initiative. All those
evoke confidence and mitigate the risk of
greenlighting something new.

And that's it. Like I said, not every project will follow this model, but most will thrive on it. So give
it a shot; hopefully, like a screenwriter starting with
an established framework, you will find it easier to
make an impact on your stakeholders.

Then, once your stakeholders are out the door and
off to do their part with gusto and heroism, wave
to them proudly and go get yourself a beer. You've
earned it.

THE BIG TAKEAWAYS
from this chapter

Mapping will take you leaps and bounds beyond
the traditional presentation outline.

Most screenwriters start with a defined mapping
structure because it makes it easier to start and
develop a compelling story. Aristotle developed the
most popular structure two millennia ago.

A dramatic story arc releases cortisol and oxytocin,
which we need to get the viewers' attention and
make them care.

There are two rails you need for a strategic story:
the emotional and the rational. The emotional
rail establishes urgency, brings in the heroes, and
builds a cause. The rational rail establishes credibility and simplifies with action.

This path gets them through the door with clarity
and desire, so they have both the rational goods
to do the job successfully (understanding) and the
desire to carry it out and recruit others (passion and
confidence).

Final Case in Point:

Verizon's Project Flow

We've got another made-up project for you, and this one is going to carry us through the rest of the book. It's called Project Flow, and it's a biggie with super-high stakes. Verizon has developed a 5G network that's many times faster and more robust than 4G LTE. So it's finally going to unleash the full power of cellular Wi-Fi, and enable us to seamlessly carry our calls, logistics, and entertainment wherever we go—from office to car to hotel and back home. Yeah, I know what you're thinking: we have that already, and hopefully, by the time you're reading this, you really will. But when I wrote this sentence in June of 2016, while carriers and device makers have promised it to us, it sure as hell ain't seamless.

But in this case study, Verizon has finally broken through the barriers and developed a network that fulfills the promise. So now it's our job to inspire all of Verizon's workforce—along with the designers and engineers at their partner companies like Google, Apple, and Samsung—to actually create this seamless experience, and most importantly, to do it right.

One caveat: Producing these fictional videos is time-consuming and expensive, so this is actually one we created back in 2010. We just haven't had the time in between projects to give it an update, so you'll see some old devices, like an iPod that most people don't use anymore. The story and videos still hold up, though, and will give us a chance to use our strategic map and give you the goods. As mentioned, each of these steps will have its own chapter and plenty of depth. Briefly, here are the steps we'll take with Verizon's Project Flow:

Welcome them in

We'll start with uplifting music and images of people using all the devices that would run on the network, in all kinds of typical settings, so we quickly get everyone into the world of mobile devices.

Create urgency & credibility

We'll pump the opportunity and establish credibility by having experts talk about how quickly consumers adopt new technology. We'll then mention and graph out the gap in the current product landscape that's leaving consumers unsatisfied. We'll then bring back the experts to talk about the boatload of money that will be made by whoever fills that gap. And finally, to ratchet up the urgency even more, we'll end with a challenge statement that reminds us that our competitors will also be trying to win the prize.

Bring in heroes

We'll frame the story in human terms by introducing a hero named Max whom everyone can relate to. Max will be handpicked from Verizon's "Blender" market segment that is most apt to adopt the Flow technology. We'll show enough of Max's personality for everyone to like him.

Simplify with action

We'll follow Max through all kinds of situations where his technology falls short of his aspirations. As we see him fumble, we'll feel his hope, disappointment, and shame. And because our stakeholders have no doubt been in similar situations, we'll bring them right back to their feelings and frustration about technology.

Evoke a cause

We'll have Max tell us how much better his life would be if only he had some of the very things we're developing.

Then we'll outline the mission to help Max and challenge our stakeholders to make it happen. We'll list the initiatives, partnerships, and assets they can tap into, so they know they don't have to start from scratch. And we'll close it out with encouragement, a little pressure, and the The Isley Brothers' "It's Your Thing," a song that will become Project Flow's rallying anthem.

In all my years on the planet, I've never found anyone who could sit still while listening to that song.

CHAPTER 6

Get 'Em Out of the Conference Room

and into the world of your story

Back in Chapter 1, we talked about how tough it is to grab attention these days—remember the goldfish with the longer attention span than you? Dr. Paul Zak gave us the neurological explanation:

> "Attention is a scarce neural resource because it is metabolically costly to a brain that needs to conserve resources. If something doesn't hold our attention, the brain will look for something else more interesting to do."

We all know that "more interesting" is the laptops, phones, and tablets stakeholders will bring to your presentation because they expect to be just as bored at yours as they were at their other meetings that day. This chapter is about holding their attention, reeling them in, and keeping those devices in the off position.

Stakeholders expecting to be bored is absolutely perfect for us. I don't know about you, but I love me some low expectations. If we can quickly, cleverly, and relevantly let them know that this presentation is not going to be the same-old-same-old, I'll bet we can get them out of the conference-room prison they expect and into the world of your strategic story—pesky devices or not.

Draw them into your world

This is another area where we can take our cue from movies and TV. They have the same challenge and they know how to work it. If you ever talk to a director or editor, you'll quickly see that the opening scene is one of their favorites to create. They love grabbing our attention and reeling us into their world. And I think that's the key takeaway: more than hitting us over the head, it's about putting in the hook.

Here's a perfect example of a powerful opener that does just that. I picked it because it's not only enveloping, but also literal: a camera travels in a car to the New Jersey suburbs with a character we all know: Tony Soprano.

If you're reading in paper form, the link is just above the photo of Tony. For those of you with the interactive version, just click on Tony's sweet mug on the left. Either way, play it at full screen, plug in your headphones, turn up the volume, and let David Chase & Co. hook you into Tony's world.

Play the opening to *The Sopranos*:
You'll find it at www.gettotheheartbook.com/movies

I hope you enjoyed it. Let me ask you this: while you were watching, were you thinking about the chair you were sitting in or did you feel like you were driving across the bridge with Tony? Either way, now consider that you only watched a YouTube clip on a small screen. If you were able to watch this on a big screen with real speakers like you use in a conference room, that envelopment just gets deeper and easier.

Let's talk about some of the techniques they use to get you inside Tony's head. As he's driving, there's a lot of chaotic camerawork and claustrophobic framing. There's also big puffs of smoke. These shots are showing us symbolically how anxious and hemmed in Tony feels.

About the time you see the bridge and arrive in Jersey, you're taken through Tony's history: first we see the industrial district where workers are feeding his empire. We move past the cemetery, where we probably find some of the people he's whacked. Just a few frames after that, we see Satriale's Pork Store, out of which Tony runs his enterprise. Then we see a street of blue-collar houses, not unlike where Tony probably lived back when life was simple, before he became the big boss.

Then it's up the hill into the affluent neighborhood, and into the driveway of the big, fat house that represents his current life as the big boss, and probably everything he ever dreamed about as he was coming up the ranks. It's the journey of success, so everything is rosy, right? It should be, but when we see the look on Tony's face as he gets out of the car, we know there's trouble in paradise. Something is clearly out of alignment, and that lures us in.

Now watch it again and look for all that symbolism.

Doesn't that opening sequence tell you so much about Tony and *The Sopranos*? Even watched casually without the location explanations, we still get a gut feeling from it—the camerawork, the music, the characterization. That opening was the first thing most of us ever saw of *The Sopranos*, and that hook was part of the show's success. Every episode began with it. For every single one of us that got caught up in this show and shelled out the extra $10-15 a month to watch it on HBO, this was our first glimpse into this incredible story. This is what pulled us out of our living rooms and dropped us in Tony's world.

Let's break it down
Now let's talk about what we can take away from the opening of *The Sopranos* and bring to your presentation. We'll start with the thing that probably hooked you first: the music. Fair warning: I'm going to yap about music quite a lot because I believe music is the quickest, most effective way to get your audience straight to that moment, that place, that emotion; it drops the viewer right into the world of your story. This track, *Woke Up This Morning* by A3, does the job immediately. You can have music playing when people arrive at your presentation. I always do, and every time I see a huge difference. It's an immediate surprise that signals to everyone that this is not going to be same as every other presentation they've seen that day. So they're refreshed. And it relaxes them and opens their minds.

Contrasts – like Oz and Kansas – are a bullet train for our brains.

Separating concepts makes it easier for us to distinguish, but can also signal a reason for us to be concerned.

We also have the images working to hook us in: the details of the working-class streets and cemetery; the contrast between the big house and Tony's face. Those contrasts—like Oz and Kansas—are so quick and powerful, especially when you've got an actor like James Gandolfini telling us exactly what we need to know about Tony with a few short expressions. (Man, do I miss him.) You too can have images playing on a screen when people arrive. Or big posters on easels lining their way in. Again, it's totally unexpected and draws them into the world of your insights and ideas—right away.

All these images are served up in quick, teasing cuts, so our attention spans aren't overtaxed. That's important—even if they say they're ready, stakeholders are never ready for anything dense right off the bat. So hitting them immediately with something complicated can be more than they bargained for. You need to draw them into it first, the way Chase's team eased us into *The Sopranos* with those quick cuts, or the slides of Sophia's story back in the Capital One example. If we'd started them off with the inevitable, I don't think it would have gone as well. But by drawing them in first, it became eye-opening.

Simple and emotional: head, heart, and gut

Not to say that making them think or wonder isn't also powerful. It's just that it shouldn't be complicated. Example: if you ask a simple but challenging question, then leave enough silence for them to ponder it, the suspense can actually get them to welcome themselves in. Movies and TV use these kinds of pauses all the time. They're like a magnet. Your stakeholders are silently thinking, while you're subliminally luring them into your ideas. Then, of course, when they can't take it any-more, you relieve the suspense and pay off their intrigue.

The group from my workshop with the upticking number on the big TV did that with aplomb. Making their stakeholders wonder, then revealing the numbers' meaning with a concrete and relevant payoff, then hiding them again, and finally, revealing the growth.

I found another striking example in the Heath brothers' book *Switch*. This story first appeared in a book called *The Heart of Change* by John Kotter and Dan Cohen. A purchasing manager at a manufacturing company needed to cut costs. So he visited all the company's factories to see what materials and processes they use. He found that none of the factories were consistent, costing the company tons of money. Right there, he had the information he needed and could now deliver upstairs.

But this manager knew that the top-level execs were unlikely to listen and make the necessary changes with just those facts, so he decided to deliver the information in a compelling way. He wanted to create a story and a symbol representing the inconsistency and lack of cohesion he'd uncovered. He found both a story and a symbol in a surprising place: work gloves.

Employees had been authorized to buy whatever gloves they wanted. Some cost $5, others $35. There were hundreds of variations of gloves, so he got a pair of every kind he came across. At the conference room, he laid them all out on the table—hundreds of gloves—and tagged each one with the cost. When the execs walked in, he didn't say anything. He let them look, feel, inspect, and wonder. He set up his story world, let them walk, and with his silence, he enveloped them. Then, when he held up two gloves and told them how they

were indicative of mass inconsistency and waste in the company, it hit them right in the gut, the brain—and the wallet. It was bold, meaningful, and visceral. And its impact was compounded by the suspense that came with the immediacy of seeing all these gloves and tags, but not hearing an explanation right away.

Shock and Ahhhh

Speaking of suspense and the power of taking stakeholders out of their comfort zone, there's an opening we created for a large sales meeting that was also amazingly effective at zapping everyone right into our world. Sales meetings are usually a huge investment for a company and our client had spent many, many thousands of dollars getting all their sales reps in one place. They couldn't afford to start their presentation with a whimper, like a guy getting on stage with a microphone or tapping his fork on a glass. We wanted to help them start it with a bang.

So as the sales reps were milling around, drinking coffee, eating bagels and yapping away, we…. cut the lights! Then … we waited while they recovered from the shock … then listened until they became a bit unsettled. Then, suddenly, out of nowhere, we filled a large screen with bright white light! The sales reps were transfixed on the screen and completely filled with anticipation. Finally, the white light faded into a movie of the company bigwigs (appearing as big heads on the screen), talking about how excited they are for the sales year, that they had big new ideas, and how their salespeople were going to be a critical part of them.

When the movie ended and the CEO walked onstage to give the opening address, the applause was deafening. He was a movie star. The reveal we created of him and the others onscreen turned into a roaring payoff, but it all started with the shock and suspense of cutting the lights. That immediately zapped everyone into the same head space. Then, together in darkness, they all experienced the same emotional tension. That enabled us to leverage their unified need for relief into two minutes of full transformation: individual conversations and bagels became shared tension; shared tension became unified focus.

And unified focus set them up for the unified positivity, exactly what you want for a big annual sales meeting.

Our shock-and-ahhh concept actually stemmed from the exercise we learned back in Chapter 4: empathy. We knew these reps wanted to be entertained and inspired. And just like the execs who walk into your conference room, we knew they expected the meeting to be a snoozer. They were probably talking about old times and new restaurants. Those were the "devices" we focused on defeating.

A provocative statement is another way to draw stakeholders into your story. Something bold and a little audacious, so the naysayers shake their heads and think, "you got some serious balls" or "I can't wait to wipe the floor with you." Either way, they're going to pay attention, which is the most important thing right now. But don't forget: a provocative statement means it's even more crucial to have a tangible and verifiable way to back yourself up. If you provoke, but then deliver a solid, satisfying payoff, you'll be a legend for the day. Seriously. Most execs love that kind of audacity. It feels like leadership.

Ok, now something a little more calming
Now let's go to the opposite end of the spectrum from shock and provocation. Movement can be just as enveloping when you're guiding them out of the same old and into your world.

I talked about how *The Sopranos* opening is literal. You're taken on the ride with Tony and end up at the key culmination point of the house and Tony's face. That example covered a number of miles, but you don't have to travel nearly that far. If you meet your stakeholders outside the conference room and lead them in, or even walk them from one side of the room to another, that short physical movement can have amazing power to change their perception. It will be especially pronounced if, when they get to the new location, you reveal something they hadn't been able to see before. Picture the opening scene of many documentaries about comedy or musical performers—first you see them backstage, then you follow them as they walk out onstage. The roar of the crowd gets louder and louder as you walk closer to that curtain. As a viewer, you know exactly what's going to happen when that curtain is lifted and the crowd is revealed, but it's still an emotionally lifting experience.

Much of the emotional lift comes from the movement, but it also comes from the anticipation of seeing what you cannot see right now. In this example, you're teased by the roar of the crowd. You can tease your stakeholders as well, just by talking up what they're about to experience before you reveal it.

It wouldn't seem like movement was utilized in the work glove presentation from the book *Switch*, but in actuality, it was. In fact, it incorporated all these techniques I've written about. Let's lay it out now: execs enter a room to find a table covered in work gloves (surprise, mystery); they walk around the table (physical movement); they touch the gloves (tactile, visceral detail), but they don't know why the gloves are there (mystery); the presenter stays silent, letting them wonder and become spellbound (suspense); finally, he explains the presentation (reveal), the key information that puts it all together. Simple, but wildly compelling.

You can also do a move-and-reveal on your screen. The easiest way is to copy a movie technique called the pan and reveal: first they show you something mundane, like a wall, then they move the camera across to reveal something interesting, like James Dean leaning against it. And because they lead to James Dean with the pan, he somehow becomes more intriguing.

How to do a move-and-reveal in PowerPoint:

Start in the open space, then move to reveal woman

The initial set up   Click to move the photo, then reveal

You can do that same move in PowerPoint by taking an image that's at least twice the size of the screen and doing a motion-path animation on it. Because everyone will be in a different version of PowerPoint, it's hard to say exactly where your motion-path tool is, but I'm pretty sure you'll find it in the Animation tab. Same with Keynote and most presentation applications.

Above you'll find an example. See those brackets at the bottom? In your first slide, you just see what's in the left bracket: the street. Then you click for the move to happen, the photo slides over, and the woman appears. You can also do it by dividing the photo in two, pasting each half in a different slide, then using the Slide transition. If you have to send your presentation to a number of people, this might be the way to go because it would minimize the technical risk that comes with all the different versions of PowerPoint those people might have, but you would have to get the photo cut right. Either way, the effect is cinematic and alluring.

You can also create movement through with the Zoom animation tool. Again, you must start with an image that's larger than your screen. In this case, a lot larger, because you'll need that extra resolution to zoom in and still see a clear picture. I'd say three times the size of your screen.

You start by showing the image in its entirety, then when you're ready to make the reveal, you click the zoom to home in on the area where you want your stakeholders focused. It will take some practice, but the effect can be pretty magical. Kind of like zooming the viewer in, rather than the image.

The opposite is also magical. You start so zoomed in that they can only see a small detail, then you zoom out to reveal the full picture.

You can take this effect further by staying at that zoomed level and moving around the image. This heightens the attention because you get to tease them even more. Again, it's important to make sure what you're doing is meaningful. Let's say you're talking about finding a solution or cause of something. You can use this technique to take them on the ride that you experienced before you found it. If you do it swiftly and make every stop relevant and revealing, even zipping around a spreadsheet can be alluring.

Wow—I just realized we've gone from Tony Soprano to a zipping, alluring spreadsheet. Just shows you how many ways there are to get stakeholders out of the boring conference room and into your world, where life is good, and you rule.

THE BIG TAKEAWAYS
from this chapter

5

The competition for attention is always tough, but the good news is that expectations are very low. Chances are your audience will come in figuring you're going to bore them to death. This will give your creativity even more power.

It all starts with empathizing with your audience. Using the payoff they'll get with your information is a huge way to draw them in.

Effective techniques for drawing them into your story: music, visuals, and teasing them by holding back information until the big reveal.

Even something as simple as cutting the lights before starting the projector can instantly send the message that your presentation is not going to be humdrum.

Movement can help you bring people into your world in a surprisingly powerful way. You don't even need much. For example, walking stakeholders into or around the conference room can be enough to change their state of mind.

CHAPTER 7

Create Urgency

and credibility, so they listen and relax

Now that you've hooked them in, you want your stakeholders to believe that your information is too important to ignore. That comes from raising the urgency they feel. If they ignore you, they may miss a big opportunity; worse, they might head right into some misfortune and look bad. And no one wants to look bad. Not bosses, not stakeholders, not anyone. But if we can evoke that urgency, they will listen and get what they need to make the smart moves and come out like geniuses.

At the same time, remember that you're asking them to go out on a limb, so it's important to establish credibility so they'll believe what you tell them and can take your confidence back to their teams.

Urgency makes them care.

Credibility makes them feel smart for caring.

Urgency and credibility work hand in hand, and it's key to balance the two. Urgency makes them care; credibility makes them feel smart for caring. You're not pulling one over on them. They can trust you. It will also signal to them that it's okay to tell their bosses, stakeholders, and others. Again, it's about making them look like a genius instead of a buffoon. I'm no math whiz, but I believe that your ratio of delivering genius over buffoon will determine your degree of success.

Confidence over anxiety

That leads me to another concept I firmly believe in: confidence over anxiety. If you can instill confidence in your stakeholders, your initiative will go smooth as silk and your contribution will be rewarded.

Making them anxious, on the other hand, will doom you to resistance and tough questions. That's Anxietyland, and why I so firmly stress credibility. Being credible keeps you out of Anxietyland and firmly in a far better place: Confidenceland. We'll tackle how to establish credibility in a moment, but first, let's create some urgency.

Creating urgency

Usually your stakeholders have decisions to make and you're asking them to make those decisions or get onboard with yours. Like all things emotional, creating urgency starts with empathy.

First think about what your stakeholders stand to gain emotionally if they follow your advice. I say "emotionally" because this is definitely elephant territory. For instance, while adding market share is nice, you'll create more urgency if you talk about beating a competitor.

On the other side, if you want them to help you solve a problem or avoid catastrophe, the urgency won't come from the problem itself, but from showing the pain and suffering that stems from it. Feeling that pain—or

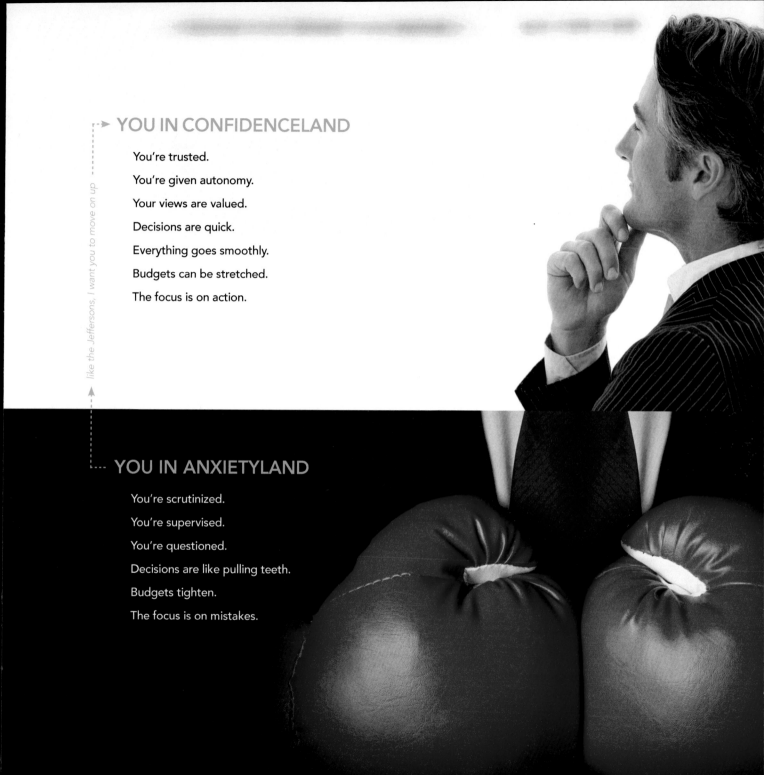

like the Jeffersons, I want you to move on up

YOU IN CONFIDENCELAND

You're trusted.

You're given autonomy.

Your views are valued.

Decisions are quick.

Everything goes smoothly.

Budgets can be stretched.

The focus is on action.

YOU IN ANXIETYLAND

You're scrutinized.

You're supervised.

You're questioned.

Decisions are like pulling teeth.

Budgets tighten.

The focus is on mistakes.

THE ALL-POWERFUL CHALLENGE STATEMENT

COMBINES THE PUSH OF FEAR WITH THE PULL OF ASPIRATION
TO MAKE ONE HIGHLY POTENT EMOTIONAL LURE

Play the challenge statement movie.
It's at www.gettotheheartbook.com/movies

fearing that it will come, continue, or grow—that's what will boost their desire to do something.

Like I said, it's all about keeping it emotional and personal, showing them people or things that we as emotional viewers care about. Not numbers or broad statements—unless you have people like experts or bigwigs in your company talk about them. That brings them back to the human level where we can feel the urgency.

If your information or opportunity allows you to combine aspiration and fear, even better. Now you have two emotions to tap, and you can bring both to a beautiful urgency crescendo.

The challenge statement

One way to reach that crescendo is with the greatest urgency button of them all: the challenge statement. A powerful challenge statement is like moving the clock from the middle of the game to right before the buzzer. Wanna see one?

Do you remember our Verizon case history? The clip to the left is our opening, but ends on a challenge statement. Here we'll establish credibility by showing experts, but what they say will be all about urgency. We'll open by talking about how big the adoption of digital is (or was in 2010) and show some examples. Then we talk about the unfulfilled need in the marketplace. An expert from *Wired* magazine will come in and say: "I don't think since the adoption of fire have we seen a steeper adoption curve."

To establish credibility, don't look just to facts and statistics. Experts are often even more influential, especially when you see them on video.

Journalists, academics, authors and execs, even from other industries, can all make fine experts.

Then we talk opportunity: "But there are so many companies in the race, it actually creates a conundrum for consumers. You have a camera, but it doesn't work with your iPad...," and then, "You have all this technology that's supposed to set you free, but what it actually ends up doing is making you feel more caged in."

Finally, we set up the big challenge statement, first by evoking our stakeholders' aspiration (and in this case, greed), and then flip it by evoking fear:

Aspiration for success
"Whoever can make all these things work together is going to have a gold mine. It's going to make someone's shareholders very, very happy."

Fear of the opposite
"The question is: who's it gonna be?"

That's the effect of a good challenge statement: huge result, up for grabs, but for how long? All these conspire to raise the need to act or see someone act.

Establishing credibility
Now that you've created a sense of urgency and made your stakeholders care about what you're saying, you also want to evoke their confidence by backing it up. Facts and data will help you here, but like in this example, you can also utilize quotes from experts or senior execs at your company. In this clip, we quoted experts from *Wired*, *TechCrunch*, and *Fortune* because they were highly credible sources at the time, but also covered different fields of expertise. With *TechCrunch* and *Wired* we would first inspire trust in our technology prediction, then *Fortune* enabled us to round it off by covering the financial side.

Here's another example of urgency and credibility: a trailer from the movie *Waiting for Superman*. It's basically a wake-up call for America about the poor state of our public school systems and a challenge to improve them. It sure moved me, even before I had a child, because it combines emotional images that make you feel a child's perspective, foreboding expert testimony, data that back everything up, and challenge statements up the wazoo. Check it out on the left.

Play *Waiting for Superman* trailer
It's at www.gettotheheartbook.com/movies

Anybody feel like that's important? Do you believe what they say? Me too. So let's look at the elements the creators used to make that happen for you.

The images are doing a lot of the heavy lifting. You have the kids raising their hands (a desire), you have the long jump (a challenge), and there's my favorite combo: the girl who first looks sweet and innocent when she's in the classroom, but then she's shown with messed-up hair and we see an image of the jail. Again, those strong contrasts.

And let's not forget the heartstrings. How can you not want to help these kids? They're so sweet and innocent, but if we don't act, we're going to lose them to Crime City. Using these emotional hooks cranks up the urgency and opens us up to empathy and cause.

And then there's the provocative statements—this trailer is full of them. My favorite: "Either kids are getting stupider every year, or there's something wrong with the educational system." He's asking us to take a stand, and that can be indescribably compelling.

Now let's talk about what makes us believe. They bring in data, but in a heartfelt way. Heartstrings and data may seem like strange bedfellows, but in truth they are a potent combination.

And of course, there's the expert testimonials. The combination of experts and data provides a ton of credibility in the minds of viewers.

When you're putting together your presentations or deliverables, keep this combination in mind so you can capitalize on the effect. If you can get your CEO or another company bigwig endorsing your case on camera, you don't even need data for people to believe. They'll see the bigwig and they'll follow. Don't settle for a typed quote, though. Do it like the movies and show that bigwig's face so stakeholders can feel the words as they hear them. That's what will move their elephants and make them feel the urgency and credibility. A typed quote just won't touch them the same way.

Both *Waiting for Superman* and the Verizon video use an evergreen emotional trick: at the moment they want to grab you and make you listen, they stop the music and create a void in the pause, then drop the killer line into the empty space. In the Verizon example, it's "Who's it gonna be?"; in *Waiting for Superman*, it's "I don't think they are, I know they are." This pause creates a magnet that sucks you in and forces you to listen. If you open your presentation with a movie, it's easy to pull off. Most stock-music tracks have a moment like that. If you're presenting live, though, you can still pull it off if you have music accompany you when you speak. It just takes precise timing and a lot of practice, but the effect is godlike in its power.

You'll have them in the palm of your hand.

THE BIG TAKEAWAYS

from this chapter

When you create urgency, your stakeholders will feel like they <u>have</u> to care.

When you create credibility, they'll feel smart for caring, and confident enough to tell other people.

Credibility helps you thrive in Confidenceland; it's so much better than getting stuck in Anxietyland.

Urgency can be supercharged by a challenge statement. What's the payoff if they take your advice? What's the cost of not following it?

You can create credibility by integrating facts, quotations from experts, and framing your points in human forms that your stakeholders can relate to.

CHAPTER 8

Bring in the Heroes

so your story will become personal and affecting

Remember those posters on your walls when you were a kid? I'll bet you had some movie and TV heroes tacked up. If you're a Boomer, maybe it was James Dean or Marlon Brando. I'm an Xer, so I had Ferris Bueller and Jeff Spicoli (you can see where my mind was). If you're a Millennial, maybe you had Katniss Everdeen or a Transformer.

Either way, if you've ever bought a product because you saw a favorite movie or TV star wearing it, using it, talking about it, or advertising it, you know firsthand the power that heroes have on all of us. Here's my confession: I bought Ray-Ban Aviators and a bomber jacket because of *Top Gun*. Feel free to laugh at me; I won't stop you.

Thankfully, I'm far too mature these days to buy stuff just because I see it on movies or TV (except for the Don Draper sunglasses I bought last year), but I still come out of every movie feeling moved, sometimes even transformed, by its heroes.

This is because the power of heroes is more than just worship and purchases. Heroes are what show and tell us the story. They're the legs on which the story moves. Heroes help us relate to a story and remember it, so they're also the teachers that help us learn.

Maverick from *Top Gun* not only broadened my awareness of sunglasses, he also taught me how awesome it is to be in the Navy. Then *Pearl Harbor* came along and I learned it wasn't nearly as awesome as I thought. Reggie Dunlop from *Slap Shot* introduced me to hockey, and the Fonz showed me that as long there's a bathroom nearby, I'll always have an office.

Most importantly, heroes are the reason we care about stories at all. They're what makes us feel "knowledgeable" enough to spout our opinions at parties and the water cooler. It's all because we saw some hero get sucked into a situation, make a few mistakes, suffer, learn, dig down deep to get past the hurdle, and then (usually) triumph. Their experiences get imprinted onto our brains. We may not realize it, but we listen more to our heroes than just about…anyone.

And that's not just me ranting on. Dr. Paul Zak has run the experiments. Dr. Paul, take it away:

> "A story with an identifiable character who has emotions is the most natural thing for our brain. By that I mean it activates evolutionarily old areas of the brain below our conscious awareness that are deeply felt and have an impact both in brain and body."

Even the anti-heroes are heroic

Heroes can even make us believe our own morals. There's a phrase I once heard: "Intimacy trumps morality." As long as we feel for them, they can still be our heroes. Take Don Draper from *Mad Men*—he's a miserable person, a horrible boss, and downright mean to the people who support him most. And yet we all root for him—and in my case, even buy his sunglasses. Here's screenwriter Kevin Marburger to tell us why:

> "The audience is always participating in the story as the main character. As long as you make that character relatable, he/she doesn't need to be likable. Walter White [from *Breaking Bad*] is a perfect example of a character who is completely relatable, but not necessarily the most likable guy.
>
> What we always like to do as screenwriters is see how much we can get away with when we plot out

our characters. Even if they make a horrible mistake or do something terribly wrong, if we can find a moment where we can bring them back, the audience will actually connect with that character even more."

Heroes at work

Heroes can bring this kind of power to corporate stories as well, by making that corporate information more personal in the same way your heroes do in a movie. With a hero, an abstract concept becomes a concrete example, and we all know how much easier it is to learn and believe when we're handed a juicy example.

Andy Cunningham, founder of Cunningham Collective and the PR legend behind the Macintosh, put it really well:

> "People like to have heroes. They crave the notion of looking up to people and they like to use their own imaginations to relate to these heroes. It gives them something to connect to, human-to-human."

But it's even more than that. When your stakeholders watch your strategy or initiative told through the lens of a hero's journey, something really cool happens. They go from relating and connecting to actually internalizing the hero,

CLASSIC HERO

COMMONALITIES:

intimacy with audience, cool sunglasses

ANTI-HERO

just like Kevin Marburger said. But Kevin doesn't have a lab, so let's get Dr. Paul Zak's take:

> "You actually begin to embody the emotions that the characters in the story have. This is your palm sweating when James Bond is dodging bullets. Once you have that emotional resonance, it's not only highly engaging from a neurological perspective, but very likely to change your behavior after the story ends."

How powerful is that—the ability to change behavior? That's communication on turbo, people. That's the power of heroes.

Now this is where people usually stop me and say, "Well, yeah, that's James Bond. He's got villains, cool gadgets and a British accent. All we have is analytics. How do we get all James Bond sexy with that?"

Let's play ball
Good question. And for you, I have two answers. The first is that you can actually make analytics sexy with a good story. Hollywood actually had a hit movie about analytics: *Moneyball* is about how analytics revolutionized baseball, and it's a great case history for us. Because long before Brad Pitt was even remotely famous, Bill James was trying to promote Sabermetrics in his books, *Baseball Abstracts*. Unfortunately, though, for Bill, it's hard to get buy-in with anything abstract, so he didn't get much traction in the MLB.

And that's how it stood for roughly 22 years. James kept publishing his baseball abstracts and kept getting ignored by the stakeholders he sought to influence. It didn't matter how smart he was or how much potential he could unlock. He just couldn't connect.

Lucky for him, he found a fan, an analyst named Paul DePodesta, who introduced it to Billy Beane, GM of the Oakland A's. They put James' concepts to work with their budget-challenged team and they began winning. Suddenly, Sabermetrics had something concrete and affecting: a story about a shoestring team doing the improbable.

And they had a hero to carry it through. Most of the glory went to Billy Beane, because it's easier for people to wrap their heads around one main hero, and as a GM willing to risk it all to do something amazing, Beane was both heroic and relatable, especially to MLB owners. And with Sabermetrics winning as well, James finally the got buy-in he deserved. He even got an exec job with the Red Sox.

But that's not all. Flash forward to Michael Lewis' book *Moneyball*, and analytics got even more buy-in (it really helps to have a great writer frame your story). Now lots of people were taking notice and Bill James even had a book written about him two years later.

Now flash forward to 2011, and analytics gets the Hollywood treatment with the movie *Moneyball*. Aaron Sorkin's screenplay took Michael Lewis' book even further.

REAL HEROES ARE EVEN MORE POWERFUL THAN ACTORS

For internal strategic stories, real people are usually more relatable than actors with a script, and definitely more credible. These people are all real (I found their photos on Creative Commons), and I'm sure they're all as heroic as any blockbuster star, and far more inspiring.

Now instead of just words, people got to see Sabermetrics in action, with all the emotion that movie-style storytelling brought to bear. The result: $110 million at the box office and millions of people watching the sophisticated power of analytics in movie-story form.

Today, analytics is a top tool in every major sport. No top GM works without them. I personally don't have the research skills to track the causality back to the movie *Moneyball,* but I do know that the timing maps out. And it's not just on the professional level. Look at the huge phenomenon that is fantasy sports, where players must, must, must have their fix of analytics. I doubt even Bill James would even disagree with me that this kind of buy-in would never have happened if sabermetrics were kept within the chipboard covers of his annual *Baseball Abstract.*

Okay, finally the second answer

The second answer is that you don't actually need a James Bond or a Brad Pitt to be your hero. The stories I've crafted in corporations over the years are usually best told with everyday heroes: consumers, employees, customers, or strategic partners. I've found that real people, who aren't camera savvy or perfectly polished, actually provide more emotional resonance in a strategic story than actors, even with all their "umms" and awkwardness. Your projects are real, so having real people as your heroes will bring you more credibility. The authenticity will also make them more relatable.

Most importantly, they'll come with relevant needs. That's really important because when your aim is to get buy-in from your stakeholders, you need to leave your story unfinished. They need a reason to go through the door—a hero they can help is far more inspiring than a hero who's got it all figured out. After all, your stakeholders are supposed to be the hero in the end—it's their payoff for joining your cause.

I like featuring a hero with the potential to be so much more if only he/she was not held back by the current state of _____ (fill in the subject of your project). Like how Taylor just wanted to be spontaneous and go to Mexico, but was held back by having to go home to get her kit. That's a need any stakeholder can relate to and feel for, and because it's unsolved, a story they can enter and support.

Our Verizon hero Max

Let's take a look at our hero Max from the Verizon project. As I mentioned, heroes are the teachers who help us learn, so Max is going to take us through the next four chapters. In insights and strategy terms, Max is the "persona" of one of Verizon's main market segments. Max's segment is called "Blenders" (the term for people who blend their work side and personal side to maximize their life experience). They're often early adopters of technology, making them perfect for a company like Verizon.

I'm sure you have some Blenders in your life. They might eke out an extra day of vacation by answering a couple of emails. Or work from home so they can get their laundry done during work hours. They can also be annoying at dinner because they have to answer every single business call.

Still, even with those personality aspects, we'll make sure there's plenty to like about Max (especially after a smooth edit). More importantly, we'll make sure there are plenty of ways to show Max illuminating exactly how and why Verizon and its partners should jump on this 5G thing and help unleash him and his fellow Blenders.

To see Max's quick intro clip, click on the frame to the right or go to the URL shown above it.

Of course, the clip isn't our hero's complete story, just an introduction. But in just twenty-seven seconds, we were able to pack in a lot of information about Max and set you up for the rest of his story. Hopefully, it made you want to get to know him more.

Play our hero Max's intro movie. *You'll find it at www.gettotheheartbook.com/movies*

As I said, we'll be going through a few adventures with Max, each showing a need that requires solving. These will help your stakeholders participate vicariously (and subconsciously) through the character of Max; if we do our job right, they'll want to create new products and experiences for him.

Rally the masses

Beyond just the presentation, Max's hero power will continue to reap dividends because your stakeholders can go back and inspire their teams around the opportunities you've identified. With Max, they'll also get to see and feel those opportunities on a human level, so they'll be even more motivated. Instead of talking about "early adopters" or "Blenders," they can tell their group of engineers, "Think about what Max was missing when he was driving to his meeting. His app kept crashing and he only had a few seconds before the tunnel." The need is now palpable for the engineers because it's so relatable.

You can supercharge the brainstorming process by focusing everyone's ideas around a hero they can relate to and feel for.

Now, instead of your people coming up with ideas for something abstract like "more relevance among professionals"— they're coming up with ideas for "Max."

Heroes and ideation

Speaking of sparking ideas, I've found that heroes are equally inspiring in ideation sessions. With an actual person like Max, you can get the group to generate ideas around him and the conflicts he wishes he could solve. You can show Max's movie or photos that lay out his story and the objects that might define Max, like his phone or baseball mitt—some kind of visual depiction of opportunity areas you want the group to ideate around.

By getting that specific, you'll see the creative process speed up and become far more enjoyable. It becomes easier because Max feels real and gives those people trying to make something out of nothing a tangible issue to focus on. After all, they just saw those circumstances and experiences unfold, so the group's ideas will be much more concrete and relevant. They're not coming up with ideas for "gaining more relevance among professionals"— they're coming up with ideas for "Max."

When I've seen ideations around heroes, the ideas generated are better and more numerous. And because everyone isn't expending so much brainpower imagining abstract concepts, I've seen groups have time and energy left to qualify their ideas with quick rankings based on criteria like how easily they can be implemented by their company or how long they'll take to get to market.

When you come home from those kinds of results, you generate more value for your company, and feel better about yourself and your work. The time and money you put toward developing a hero is so worth it.

But heroes go even further

Like we illustrated with Taylor back in Chapter 4, a hero also gives you a powerful way to socialize your initiative. Besides using images in your PowerPoint and videos, you can put your hero on posters, trading cards, anything. You can easily get an entire company, even a global one, inspired around a common hero.

Even your finance department will be able to appreciate that kind of efficiency and leverage. But I think the biggest beneficiaries are the execs with limited time. Heroes really speed up their information-sharing process and reduce the need for extended communication (i.e., more meetings).

When it's all said and done

When your initiative is implemented and your market share soars, it's time to put together your case history—one of those rare times you get to brag without looking like an ass. In your case-history, the hero can be a person, but can also be the product you took to market, the new strategy you implemented, or the policy that worked wonders. Even though it's not a person, you can still develop a dramatic arc for it, taking it through the opportunity that sparked the idea, through the development, the challenges, and the success it gained in market. And in the course of that arc, try to make heroes of everyone that contributed to its success, including you.

Especially you.

THE BIG TAKEAWAYS

from this chapter

Heroes are the reason we care about stories. We relate to them and we embody them through the story, learning lessons that shape our opinions and behaviors.

Heroes in corporate stories make your information personal, just like in a movie. And they can turn an abstract concept into a concrete example.

Heroes make it much easier to rally your teams around a project, generate ideas, or solve problems through a hero like "Max."

Real people often make the best heroes because they're more credible.

Heroes even strengthen the bottom line because they quicken the information-sharing process and reduce the need for extended communication.

CHAPTER 9

Simplify with Action

so they can see it and feel it even more

Here at Backstories, the number-one thing we're asked to do is to "bring it to life." We're always happy to do it because it's a hell of a lot of fun. It garners our clients a ton of prestige and satisfaction, and I love the way it brings our clients to life as well. Seeing clients who have lost their excitement for a long, drawn-out project suddenly get reanimated? That makes me happy. Kid-at-Disneyland happy.

But then, I guess you could say it's in my blood—turns out my surname "Frank" actually stems from "Frankenstein" (yup, true story). So yeah, I'm all about bringing things to life. And my favorite way to do it is through action.

In movie terms, action is any movement, or even a portrayal of thought, like a gaze out a window. It's all action because it <u>shows</u> us what's going on, rather than telling us.

That's even more important in the business world, where concepts are more complex. Showing, rather than telling, saves everyone time and work. For instance, when you have something hyper-complex like a strategic model, you can spend 15 minutes walking people through it, but often they still won't really understand it. If you can show it through action, you can cut that time down to three minutes and more people will get it, and in the same way. They no longer have to visualize it internally and come up with a different visual than the person sitting next to them.

And just like with the visual, the dividends of showing action increase when your stakeholders have to present the strategic model on their own to their teams. They'll be able to show your model more accurately and with less time and effort. Anytime you can spare people time and effort (especially time-crunched executives), while increasing synergy in the company, you're providing your company a ton of value.

But it's not just about making it easier. Showing action will also help you communicate more deeply because it gets you that one-three punch. If we see it, we'll feel it. Or as Dr. Keith Oatley, Professor Emeritus of Cognitive Psychology at the University of Toronto, puts it:

> "We experience our own emotions in the circumstances that occur with the character's actions."

That isn't to say that you always have to do it in video form or show it live. Dr. Carl Plantinga, Professor of Communication Arts and Sciences at Calvin College, found that even still images and sounds are also capable of instilling deep understanding:

> "Psychologists and biologists have discovered over and over again that the mirror neurons are activated not merely when actions are seen and heard, but also when moving photographic images and recorded sounds of action are seen and heard. In part, this accounts for the affective power of the audio-visual media."

That in mind, let's start with the most basic form of action.

Finding action in a still slide

Remember earlier when we covered how to take raw data and find your characters, settings, and plot? Action is just the experience of those things. It's something happening, somewhere, to someone. It doesn't have to be Tom Cruise flying out of an exploding helicopter. It can be someone holding an opinion, buying something, or being in a position to capitalize on an opportunity.

Again, it all starts with this Mad Lib from Chapter 3—look at your data point, then think to yourself:

For example, _____ .

Now you've got action.

Now that we've got action, let's show it

So in its most basic form, building your slides in a simple story (like Puppy Claus in Chapter 3) creates action.

You then take it further by presenting a photograph that shows action, like Dr. Plantinga talked about.

You can also increase your action with the movement we discussed in Chapter 7 with the photo of the woman on the street. When you're taking people through a strategic model, for instance, you can show each section one at a time, but then use a sliding transition instead of a normal click to create that action of moving to the next section of the model. To make it feel real, though, you need to have a piece of your model on the first slide extend off the right edge, then on your next slide, have it shift to appear on the screen. When I animate the visual that opens up Chapter 2, that's what I do and it feels completely fluid. The subway starts as the hairy mess, then slides to the left and becomes the straight set of tracks you see on the following page. Similarly, if you talk about sales going up, you can animate that number to physically move up as well. Just don't get too gimmicky with it.

A more advanced way to show action is across a series of visuals, like we did with Capital One. The key is to have a central hero, like Sophia, so it's easier for people to follow.

If you can't shoot your own action sequence, you can sometimes find them in stock photo sites like *istock.com* or *dreamstime.com*. Once you find a good shot, look for a link somewhere below the photo that says "more with this model." If you click on it, you'll find shots from the whole photo session, most featuring your hero. And since photographers think in stories, there's a chance you might get the whole sequence you need. That will save you from hunting for shots individually, and will give you that central hero that ties it all together.

Now let's see Max in action

Video is an even more powerful way to show action, and since it's digital, it's also an easy way to socialize it around your company. In fact, now that we've gotten to know Max a bit, let's continue our Verizon 5G story and follow Max's adventures so you can get acquainted with action's full effect. You'll see this action sequence by clicking on the photo on below or following the URL.

Play the action movie
at www.gettotheheartbook.com/movies

A bit of warning: this clip is super painful. Max is going to have a very, very difficult time integrating his devices. It's also where the old technology really shows, but the action is still relevant to today's experience.

Action simplifies everything, while simultaneously making the experience more powerful.

Painful, right? But you know why it's painful? Because you felt it. Now imagine your stakeholders are the folks responsible for designing the dashboard electronics for that car. If you're them, you're feeling that pain even more, and because you want to alleviate the pain, you've probably already come up with four or five ideas to help Max. Why? Because the action of the scene made you experience and feel his frustration, and being a good, feeling person, you wanted to save him. (Plus you're the designer, so it's your job.)

That's what an action sequence does for people. It takes us right to the event, clears up ambiguity by directly showing us what's going on, and makes us feel the characters' emotions.

Seriously, if I'd made you read about Max's troubles instead of showing you this clip, would you have understood the experience even half as well? Or half as quickly? Of course not. Because action is the ultimate simplifier. It clarifies the complex, while simultaneously making the experience of clarity more powerful.

B-roll: action's impersonator
If you cannot be there for the action, Hollywood also has a handy technique called "B-roll." They call it B-roll because it's shot with the B camera. The A camera is the one they use to shoot the actors or the interviews you see in a documentary.

It works like this: viewers hear the voice of your killer quote, but instead of seeing the person speaking, they see images or footage that realistically or symbolically show what the quote is describing. Done well, it creates the same effect as seeing the action itself. Sometimes it's even more influential because your stakeholders will feel as though the person is speaking directly to them, or as if they're reading that person's mind.

Let's run a B-roll example, but first let's see the quote without it. The clips below have a quote that Verizon's marketing department would salivate over. Max is going to tell us exactly why his life as a Blender is so much better. Click on the photo on the bottom-left corner to hear the quote.

Pretty good quote, right? Now let's try it with some B-roll. Click the photo on the bottom-right to see the B-roll fly.

Isn't that so much more illustrative? Here's the story behind it: we shot that quote while we were in Napa with Max. It was the last shot of the day and we were all super hungry, including Max. So we couldn't ask him to trudge back to San Francisco to shoot the scene in his office. We're cruel taskmasters, but not that cruel.

So instead, we went to a restaurant, and thought about what kinds of shots could symbolically capture the office part of his quote. As we waited for our food, we pulled out a laptop and asked Max to start typing. We shot his hands on the keys because we knew if we got in close enough, the shot could still look like he was at his office, even though it was shot in the restaurant. Then, to evoke his stress, we shot a close-up of his face, looking down toward the keys, and of course, his buggy, twitchy eyes. And just like that—voila—the power of B-roll enabled us to fake our way to action and still eat.

Remember "contrast" back in Chapter 4 when we talked about Kansas and Oz? In this case, Kansas is the office, and Oz is Napa. So when Max talks about the office, we show those two claustrophobic shots of his hands and buggy eyes; when he talks about the free-

NO B-ROLL

Play the movie with no B-roll
You'll find it at www.gettotheheartbook.com/movies

WITH B-ROLL

Play the movie with B-roll
It's also at www.gettotheheartbook.com/movies

dom and ease of being a Blender, we switch to Napa and see him in that gorgeous vineyard. The visual contrast allows us to emphasize the emotional contrast that Max feels, and helps you feel it, too.

In movie-form, B-roll has one other benefit. If you check the two clips, the one with B-roll is actually seven seconds shorter than the one without B-roll—a huge benefit to a time-strapped executive. That's because B-roll allows you to edit out the "ummms" and long pauses by covering them up with the visuals. It will even let you switch the sentence around if you want, or grab audio from a completely different place. Movies, especially documentaries, do that all the time because it helps move the story along and allows for more options—while completely hiding the edits from the viewer.

B already rolls for you

We've touched on this, but let me reinforce it: you can use B-roll in your PowerPoint presentations as well. See that big screen where you project your slides? That's your B-roll canvas. So in addition to putting up action shots that you can point to and talk about directly, you can also put up images that indirectly reinforce your words. Just like we did for Max, the effect is the same. The images gets your stakeholders into the action, and your voice goes right into their head, like a thought. This will help you illustrate your points and come across with even more authority.

Framing your action

The way you "frame" or compose your shots also shapes the emotional experience. Close-ups are about intimacy. Beads of sweat, tears, breath—all make us feel what the characters feel. On the other extreme, wide shots give us a huge sense of free-

The Punch In

Play an example of the Punch In
at www.gettotheheartbook.com/movies

dom, or can also make us feel the vulnerability of the characters when they're framed in a huge expanse.

Framing can also help you increase the action and emotion. Like the zoom from Chapter 6, there's a technique called the "punch in." It's meant to jolt us, which is perfect for the emotion we want to enhance with the punch in of Max.

In our Verizon story, Max experiences an awkward phone call with his wife. We wanted to accentuate Max's embarrassment, so we alternated between a wide shot and a close-up version of the same shot. If we did our job right, then it should help you feel Max's awkwardness, and in the process, feel even more for Max. Click on the picture of Max to the left (or go to the URL) and let us know how we did.

Just like those zooms, though, you have to start with more resolution so the picture still holds up when you punch in. For instance, if you shoot at full HD (1920x1080, also known as 1080p) and play it on the web at 720p, you can stretch your image 50%. But if you're projecting it on a big TV, you might not have that room. So definitely watch it at the desired resolution to make sure it looks professional.

First try using action just to make your point clear by taking your stakeholders to the event, like we did with Sophia. Then, when you're ready for more, think about action as a tool for emotional effect. And please: use all your newfound power for the good of humanity.

THE BIG TAKEAWAYS

from this chapter

Action simplifies things because the stakeholders no longer have to read. They can see, hear, and even feel it.

Action doesn't have to be explosive. It can be just the experience of characters, settings, and plot. All those show us a lot more than you'd think.

You can find action in your data and with the "for example_____" Mad Lib from Chapter 3. The action will come.

Action can be shown in photos, but it's even more impactful in video.

Treating the screen behind you as a B-roll canvas can also help you create action without actually having the real thing there, and it will make you even more authoritative because your voice will be in your stakeholders' heads.

CHAPTER 10

Build The Cause

so they'll run with your ideas

Now that you know how to deliver the facts while stirring people up in the process, your presentation needs one final push to the finish line. It's time to evoke a feeling of cause in your stakeholders. Evangelize them into your mini-revolution so they'll pick it up and run with it.

To do that, we'll need to bring everything together into a nice little package so your new apostles can carry it down the hall and use it to inspire their teams.

The basics of the cause are not that different from the conclusion paragraph of a junior-high essay, but a lot more sophisticated and powerful. It encapsulates the most important facts and inspires everyone to evangelize them. Think of those rousing movie and TV speeches where politicians and lawyers bring everyone over to their cause: Jimmy Stewart in *Mr. Smith Goes To Washington*, Kevin Costner in *JFK*, Sam Waterston's character on *Law & Order*. They're basically doing the same thing as an eighth grader—funneling their points toward a final statement. But if I'm ever on trial, I'll take Jack McCoy over an eighth grader, so let's start stealing from the masters: their screenwriters and speechwriters.

There are a couple of key ways they do this. Instead of voicing facts, screenwriters and speechwriters voice impact, story, and emotion. And just like we've been doing all along, they talk on a human level, making it concrete and personal so everyone feels their words. They frame their facts in easy-to-remember phrases that evoke images—like Martin Luther King, Jr. interspersing scenes of white and black children sitting together at a table, and putting a bow on it with the repeated phrase "I have a dream." That fusion of vivid scenes and a rallying call evoked a cause in everyone, so in the end, the dream wasn't just his. Johnny Cochran was certainly no MLK, but he did use the same tenets to pull off something pretty incredible at the O.J. Simpson trial: he made everyone forget weeks of expert testimony by trotting out the simple visual of a glove and one memorable phrase: "If it doesn't fit, you must acquit."

You, my friends, actually have a huge advantage over lawyers and movie stars making all those big speeches. In movies, the camera holds on the hero's face and hands, rarely cutting away to other images; in the courtroom, they're also on their own. But you have a big screen behind you that can light up with images, movies, and audio elements that bring your stakeholders back to your big story and cement them for good.

Mr. Smith was one of many movie heroes who was exceptional at voicing a cause.

You can be like Beyoncé at Madison Square Garden. And for all you lazy people out there like me: you don't even need to look for new images, because you can actually reuse the ones you've already gathered for your other sections. Yay laziness!

Here's the formula I use most often to construct a cause:

1. Recap your heroes' aspirations and wishes.

2. Highlight the gaps between those aspirations and the current situation.

3. Show the pain caused by those gaps and the workarounds your heroes are forced to use—the more clumsy and frustrating, the better.

4. State that there are opportunities to close those gaps and relieve the hero's pain. Include your heroes' suggestions, always crediting it to them.

5. Express the payoff of being the successful stakeholder who champions this idea, and of course, the dividends it will pay the company. If it will crush your competitors, even better.

6. Outline what your stakeholders already have going for them to help capitalize on those opportunities.

7. Emphatically encourage them to go for it.

Phrasing your opportunities to be bold, but still keeping you out of trouble

The closing section is, of course, when you're supposed to make recommendations. But recommendations can often be risky. People may feel threatened, like they're being told what to do, or fearful of more work being dumped on their plates. Other times, your recommendations might be improperly utilized, and yet you can still get blamed.

What if, instead, we flipped the recommendation into more inviting phrases like "Imagine if…?" or "What if…?" Just like I did to open this paragraph. Or like this:

> "Imagine if Ted (our hero) didn't have to take out the garbage every week. What if the garbage could take itself out?" Then cut to Ted hauling filthy cans, saying, "That would make my life so much better." (And believe me, it would. I can't wait 'til my kid gets old enough to take it over.)

"Imagine if"s allow you to say pretty much the same thing as a recommendation, but rephrase it into an invitation for your stakeholders to grab the glory of a solution. It's a simple twist, but can make your message even more inspiring and empowering while reducing your risk of blowback.

Ending in Confidenceland

Speaking of risk, whenever the stakes are high, so is the feeling of risk and anxiety. That's just the way it is. But you need your stakeholders to feel confident when they back you. This is where I've found #6 really helps. Listing other efforts, assets, or partnerships you can leverage really helps minimize the feeling of risk, because you're telling them, in effect, they're not alone and that things are already heading in that direction so all they have to do is hop onboard.

The last step to building your cause is the short, galvanizing rallying cry that people can print on T-shirts and posters, etc., or even just repeat to their teams when they're relaying your information. This is your chance to be MLK, JFK, or anyone ending with a K. It doesn't even have to be super-witty. There's nothing poetic about Nike's "Just do it," but it was short and simple, and that's what gave it the ability to be repeated, and in turn, infused it with power.

Then, the last critical step. Show your entire cause section to an objective outsider (or insider if it's confidential). Present it the same way you will when you're in front of your stakeholders. Then ask them the same question I asked back at the ad agency: "What did you get from it?" Not: "Did you like it?" but "What did you get from it?" Then ask your listener if they want to join your revolution. They'll always tell you "yes," so listen mostly to their level of urgency. If they say it quickly and emphatically, you'll know you have the power.

Crafting the cause for Max
When we created our fake Verizon story, we wanted to make it as challenging as possible on ourselves (every day is boot camp here at Backstories), so we chose the most difficult scenarios: many different stakeholders, various opportunity areas, no easy narrative, politically touchy. All the lovely little goblins you could possibly experience.

We figured each key stakeholder would focus on one or two points. So we chose to make our points quickly and with uniform emphasis, then presented a rallying cry that would inspire all our stakeholders to contribute to a unified rollout, kind of like tentacles pushing a squid. Here's how it went:

1. Recap our hero's aspirations
Max wants his digital experiences to flow with his life. As he says, "I just want it to be … where everything flows and I feel like the real me. Out in the world, where everything is happening, but still make it my own, you know what I mean?"

2. Highlight the gaps between aspirations and the current state
Here we show what can be fixed, but phrase it with "imagine if" so it feels more inspiring: Imagine if Max didn't need to worry about...

- Leaving DVDs at home

- His phone not syncing

- His calls not connecting

- His music being hard to find

- His navigation system being one more thing he has to learn

Innovation opportunities lie in the gaps between what heroes could experience and what's currently holding them back.

The opportunities to market those innovations lie in the pain felt by those gaps.

3. Show the pain those gaps cause

With each of those items above, we also show a photo that brings you back to that scene, a specific reminder of the pain Max felt.

In truth, we were more subdued than I would normally be. The reason is that when you see the movie put together, you'll see that our cause section comes right after the scene we talked about in the last chapter, where we accentuated Max's awkwardness with the punch in. Right after that, Max puts down the phone and says: "Well, that little mishap's going to cost me." Max's line speaks boldly to the kind of pain every stakeholder can relate to and empathize with. So since our cause section comes no more than two seconds later, we figured that pain was still lingering, so we could move on to the opportunities that will relieve Max's pain.

4. Show opportunities to close the gaps and relieve the pain

Here we say, "With Project Flow, we can unleash the Maxes of the world and create value for them like they have never seen." Then we feed their dream machine, again using our key word, "Imagine … " Here's what we say:

> "Imagine a store that feels like a Bond Street tailor, with a whole portfolio of products that enable the Flow lifestyle."

Once we have painted the dream for them, we make it more concrete by including wireframe graphics of the products they would expect, and some they wouldn't. Wireframes are the beginning stages of the design process, so they're incomplete, making them inviting. Then we take them back into dreamland with ideas that will feel aspirational for them.

5. Express the payoff of being successful, both for the company and for themselves

Here we remind them of the upside for the company: "Blenders like Max represent an $8 billion market and are highly influential … they are the most interested in digital integration … they are the perfect evangelists for Flow."

Play *the Cause section of our Verizon movie. You'll find it at www.gettotheheartbook.com/movies*

6. Outline what they already have going for them

Here's where we try to alleviate the fear of starting from scratch. There's always fear in anything that requires a ton of work and money. So we make sure to mention that partners like Apple and Google will support the initiative financially by paying for the hardware and software. Then we talk about how Verizon will support the project. We include:

- The new 5G network already in development (always good to leverage existing investments) that makes it super speedy and reliable

- The partnerships, so we don't have to go it alone

- The stores that will sell the technology and the lifestyle for Verizon

- The brand (us) that can make it all happen

7. Encourage them to go for it

We close it out by showing Max in his car, ready to bust out of there, while the Isley Brothers' anthem "It's Your Thing" revs it up even more. The closing line: "Unleash the Blenders of the world."

Finally, the Verizon logo pops up, then "Go Flow"—our short, simple rallying cry.

These scenarios don't sound too impactful when you read them, so click on the frame to the left to see the actual movie version.

The two goods they need most when they get through the door

With your story now laid out, your stakeholders stand at the door with the two things that will make them capable, confident, and inspired—enough to carry our torch, lead their teams, and succeed.

They'll have clarity: what's happening and who it's happening to (and where), all the opportunities, and how to capitalize on them, as well as all the information they'll need to lead and answer questions.

And they'll also have what few others give them: the desire to mobilize their teams and create innovative ideas to help your heroes.

By moving your stakeholders' elephants, you will not only help them lead, but completely differentiate yourself from all the other presentations they'll see that day, or even that month.

You'll make a bigger difference and see real impact of your work and thinking. Exactly the kind of stuff that will get you a regular seat at their table.

THE 5 BIG TAKEAWAYS
from this chapter

Wrap your Cause section like a gift your stakeholders can take with them and evangelize to others—just like the last paragraph of a classic five-paragraph essay, but frame it with your hero in need so it will affect them emotionally.

Again, be simple and visual, like MLK or Johnny Cochran. "If it doesn't fit…"

Flip the classic recommendation to something more inviting like "Imagine if…?" or "What if…?" That lets stakeholders envision the solution and reduces the risk of backlash.

Look for other initiatives, assets, or partners you can leverage so your stakeholders won't feel like they're going it alone.

Just like in Chapter 2, run your Cause section by someone not involved in the project and ask what he or she got out of it and if they'd want to join up. If the "yes" comes with enthusiasm, you're there.

CHAPTER 11

Perform like a Keynote

with your new secret weapon for captivating

First of all, congratulations—you now have your Masters in movie-style story-telling for business. You know how to simplify information and tell it in a way that's both strategic and inspiring. You know how to create urgency, credibility, inspirational heroes, and action. You've come so far so fast. Your mom and I are so very proud of you.

Now comes the super-fun part: presenting it all like a keynote-level speaker. The kind of experience where you have stakeholders and conference audiences in the palm of your hand, where they tweet that they're sitting in one of the best talks of the year, when they congratulate you afterward, and then ask you how you got to be so good at public speaking.

Yes, you can be this good. While it helps to have a dynamic personality, even that's not required. Ask anyone I work with or live with and they'll tell you I'm a bumbling moron. I'm also a bad driver, I walk funny, and I always forget something when I leave my house or office. Always. That's my baseline, and I'll bet Jerry Seinfeld and Beyoncé have theirs as well. So believe me, it doesn't matter where you start. Flaws and all, it is 100% possible for you to get to that keynote level.

What does it take?

The desire and dedication to do what all the top comedians, pop stars, and keynote speakers do: own your content and prepare it well enough to put on a show.

Here's the bad news: Yes, it takes many, many hours, which is why I put this chapter in the high-stakes section of the book. You don't have to do it every time. But for those big presentations you give once or twice a year, or when you speak at a conference, your mom and I both know you can do it.

Here's the good news: Not only will you get buy-in for your ideas, you'll feel like a god. I know I do, and it totally makes up for all the hours I put in, the heckling and honks I endure every day, and all those emails and calls that never get returned. All those things that make me feel like crap get immediately rectified. It's that good.

So in this chapter, I'm going to tell you how I prepare for my workshop and conference presentations. It's a lot like some of the tips you'll find in a Google search, and

I recommend doing that as well, but I'll try to be more substantial and personal than your usual top-5 list.

Then I'll give you the big technique I never see in Google searches. It's one I learned from the movies and the one tool that takes me completely over the edge with my audiences.

Ready? Let's do it.

Preparing a rock star presentation

Every captivating presentation starts with captivating content, put together in a captivating way. Lucky for us, we've already done that. If you followed the map, you've got your slides and movies set up in a lean, clear, emotionally affecting way. You've got your story. Now let's make it sing.

Step 1: Make two versions

If you're giving an internal presentation or a pitch to a key client, at some point you'll probably be asked for more depth. Hopefully, that will always be the case, because it shows they're interested. Knowing that's coming, though, could very well put a voice in your head that keeps saying, "You have to include this." That voice is understandable, logical, and possibly correct. Unfortunately, it will also weigh down your presentation and performance. So I suggest honoring that need in a way that will actually serve you: make two versions. The first version is the one you present; the longer second version is given to people as a leave-behind or if they request it. Now you're able to put your real but nagging worries into a format that people can read at their leisure, and it will be on paper, which is so much easier on their eyes than a screen. It's what Nancy Duarte would call a "Slidedoc."

Speaking of Nancy Duarte, whose company, Duarte Design, has created more high-stakes keynote presentations than anyone, let me now cite her on why that long-text version should stay on the Slidedoc and not appear on your screen.

I mentioned this back in Chapter 1, but Nancy's been at this longer than me and has crafted presentations for people like Al Gore, so I'm going to piggyback on her credibility here. In her book, *Slide:ology*, Nancy reports that when presenters read the text on their slides aloud (which they always do), it actually hurts their message—the audience tends to read faster than the speaker can speak. So when your stakeholders hear a different set of words than their eyes are trying to read, it makes it difficult for them, and most likely annoying.

So please listen to Nancy and me and keep your onscreen version simple and visual. Use the B-roll technique we talked about in Chapter 9 so your audience can get the words from your voice, where you will evoke a great deal more authority.

Lastly, aim for your onscreen presentation to run no more than 50% of the time you've been allotted. That way you can accommodate all the extra questions, interruptions, technical problems, and anything else that might pop up. And most important: it will free you from the insidious clock in your head that makes you race through your presentation.

Keep your presentation to no more than 50% of the time you've been allotted.

That way you can accommodate extra questions and interruptions.

But most importantly, you won't have to race through it.

TEXT VERSION I GIVE AS A LEAVE-BEHIND

Context gives everyone the same key takeaways

If you ask ten different people what's going on here, everyone will have the same idea. Because you've given them the context of kids playing in a muddy mess. They can see the mud, they can see that the kids are in their early teens, they can feel the crazy importance because they can see it on the blond kid's face. And because they can also see the ball, they know why it's important.

VERSION I SHOW ON SCREEN AS B-ROLL FOR MY VOICE

I usually write the text version first, then use the text on my slides as the starting point of my script. Or if I already have a compelling way of talking about a slide, I'll do the opposite and place the words from my mind onto my text version and then refine it. Either way, I make sure that the text version and my script align.

Starting with the text version also forces me to do something that seems counterintuitive: it helps me find better visuals. Like most things, simple is usually better, and when you have to put text on an image, it forces you to find a simple visual that doesn't compete with it—like our Sophia images, where the visual focus was on the right and the area on the left was free for our stats. If I can't find an image with that available space, I put a white box under the text so it's readable, then set the transparency at around 10% so you can see the photo underneath, but the text is still legible.

I'm not saying all your visuals need to be this simple, especially if you're going to point to that visual and use it as a discussion topic.

But if you're only using it allegorically—like if you're talking about emotional design and show the tailfin of a 1930s car. A more simple reference like that provides that visual understanding far more quickly, so your audience will go back to looking at you.

Step 2: Make it cinematic

Now that you've made your presentation visual, it's time to go further by thinking about how your slides will move. This is another point I got from Nancy's book, *Slide:ology*: adding movement both in terms of how your slides are animated and how they transition from one to the next.

This starts as simply as our Puppy Claus slide from Chapter 3. By having only one thing on your slide appear at a time, it keeps it simple and creates movement just by the way the screen changes with each addition, and that keeps people engaged.

You can increase that engagement by making those moves reinforce your message and enhance its meaning (like the methods we discussed in Chapters 6 and 9), but here's another example. When I animate the slides on the left, I don't reveal the ball until I talk about "why" they're doing what they're doing, because the ball is the key to the why. Similarly, when I animate the guy on page 81, I start with a visual of just his head, and at the same time say, "Hit them in the head." Most people think it's going to end there, but then I say "Hit them in the gut," while I slide the picture down to reveal his gut, as if I had tilted a camera. And when I say "heart," I do a similar tilt. It's a sequence that creates cinematic movement, increases understanding, and keeps people engaged, in the way I want.

When I transition between slides, I ask myself if a simple click would work, or if it would be more effective with a fade, a slide, a flip, or something else. For instance, when I talk about my point in the previous chapter about flipping the recommendation into the "imagine if," I use a flip transition when I say the word "flip." (Which brings up another suggestion: when you use transitions, try to use phrases that suggest visual movement—like the word "flip.") I always start a simple click, though, so I don't overuse the fancy transitions and diminish their impact.

Step 3: Show it to your elite team of objective editors

As discussed in Chapters 2 and 10, my next step is to run it by people who know the material about as well as the folks I'll be speaking to, and who will also give me good, honest, ruthless feedback. In my case, it's my co-workers and my wife. But if I'm creating something fresh and big, like a new workshop, I'll invite colleagues and clients and give them lunch and cocktails. Nothing fuels honesty like cocktails.

This practice always helps me trim and fine-tune the presentation and gives me great ideas. I might end up switching the order around or adding slides or ideas, but mostly it helps me kill the evil babies that hold me back. Whatever makes it speak more clearly, I go for it.

Step 4: Stand up for yourself and your ideas

Gestures and facial expressions are also powerful ways to emphasize your points. For people to see them, though, you'll need to stand in front of the screen. That's where you should be anyway, because that's where your credibility is born. Your stakeholders will know they're listening to someone confident enough to stand in front of them. It will also enable them to keep their eyes and ears in one part of the room, which they'll really appreciate, and helps you keep their attention.

Step 5: Rehearse and memorize
When I go to a conference, I always go to the sessions and watch the speakers. I cannot tell you how many I see glued to their podium, looking at their screen or down at their notes, reading them like it was the first time they'd seen their presentation. Everyone in the audience is nice and polite for a while, and then...the laptops come out, but not to take notes. I see email, solitaire, eBay, ESPN, I've even seen porn, but never, ever notes.

When I see the main keynote speakers, I witness the complete opposite. They're looking at us, directly at us, and never at their slides or script. They're so much more engaging and the room absolutely blooms with energy. And because the speakers are looking us in the eye and clearly know their information inside and out, the audience also believes the words they say. We simply cannot deny the authority the keynotes bring.

So instead of laptops and phones, the audience forms a line to shower the speaker with adoration. They buy their books. They tell everyone how amazing it was.

What's the biggest difference? Some of it stems from the speaker's experience, absolutely. But mostly, it's that those speakers take the time to memorize their presentations and rehearse them until they can look us in the eye and give us that level of performance.

When I have a big presentation coming up, I rehearse it at least 25 times beforehand, sometimes 50. I practice until I can say it not just by heart, but with complete confidence. And I rehearse the first minute at least 80 times. I do full-on rehearsals in my office before anyone shows up, or in my garage, always standing up like I do when I present, always with my clicker and the screen showing. But I also do mumble rehearsals when I go for a walk, in my car, or in the bathroom. I record it and listen to myself to see if I can hit points even better. Then I practice more. The entire thing 25-50 times, and the beginning, at least 80.

Then, on the day of my presentation, I stop practicing, so when it's showtime, I'll sound loose and off-the-cuff.

Step 6: Know your room and equipment
If you have access to the room where you'll be speaking, spend some time there—get to know it so you'll feel comfortable. If you can, do some rehearsals there so you feel at home and familiarize yourself with the equipment. If you don't have advance access to the room, like at a sales call, see if you can find out what kind of hookups they have, then ask the client if you can come 30 minutes early to set up. If you're speaking at a conference, ask for a technical check as early as you can. In any of these situations, always bring your own computer, clicker, and whatever adapters you need to hook up to projectors with HMDI, VGA, and DVI. I emphasize this because technical issues can drive you absolutely nuts, so if you can nail them down, it's one less crazy-maker you need to worry about.

Step 7: Fending off nervousness

Does rehearsing, memorizing, showing up early, knowing the room and the equipment alleviate nervousness? No. At least it never does for me. I'm always nervous. But having everything nailed down does alleviate a lot of stress, which is just as important. And all that practice? Well, this is where the practice really pays off.

Remember how I practiced my opening around 30 more times than the rest of my presentation? It's now so embedded in my head so deeply that it doesn't matter how my nerves feel—my mouth has been trained to say all the right things.

So when I step on stage, for those first 15 seconds or so, I am pure machine. My heart is racing, but my mouth is on autopilot, so even though I'm nervous as hell, I can still hear my words coming out perfectly. I can also see everyone reacting positively, and at that point, I start to feel the shift. My nerves calm down, my heart goes back to normal, and I'm able to take control of my mouth again. This is when I feel absolutely amazing. It's like I have two experiences at once—I can concentrate on people in the audience and yet my words are still flowing on their own. I can even think about a gesture I'm going to use in about a minute. All because I've rehearsed so much. That's the payoff for all those hours of preparation. And it's so worth it.

Step 8: Give yourself breaks

Another advantage to including videos into your high-stakes presentations (like the Verizon sample from earlier) is that they give you nice breaks here and there to relax, get yourself a sip of water, take a glance at the audience, and enjoy yourself.

Because I've practiced my opening so many times, it doesn't matter how nervous I am.

My mouth is a trained machine and says all the right things.

**Play my favorite
performance tool**

You'll find it at
www.gettotheheartbook.com/movies

Step 9: Answer questions fully, even if it's tomorrow

Final step: always leave plenty of time for Q&A, especially in an internal presentation. This is why I have the 50% guideline. And be prepared to get questions you did not anticipate. This will probably fluster you like it does most people. Here's what I do: admit you don't know the answer and that you need to get back to that person. Whenever I've done that, it's so much better than providing a half-assed answer on the spot. It also gives you a chance to speak one-on-one with them later on, where you can really talk, satisfy their curiosity, and foster the relationship.

If the Q&A peters out prematurely, I'll often ask my own question: what resonated with you most about what I said? That always starts a new round of discussion and prompts new questions.

And now, my favorite tool of all

There's an element you can include in your presentation that is so powerful, it can take you to a mythic level. You've seen it in every great movie, and it's probably one of the biggest reasons you love your favorite films, even though you'll never see it on the movie poster.

Actually, I believe this magical ingredient is even more omnipresent. I think it's the key ingredient in everything we humans find interesting.

See that photo of the roaring crowd on the left? Click on the play button or go to the URL. Again, grab your headphones and turn it up.

You are about to feel this secret ingredient down to your toes...

...

...

...

..Tension

Tension, as I say in the video, is hardwired into our brains, our hearts, and definitely our guts. It's why we love the thrill of driving fast, the sway of dancing, the challenge that comes before an accomplishment, or that tick, tick, tick of a roller coaster heading slowly up the track before....

...the big drop.

Tension is what lures us to the sting of hot sauce, the sour before the sweet, and of course, it's the key aphrodisiac in the grand poobah of them all: sex. Without the tension in the lead-up to that glorious climax, would the happy ending be as good? Of course not. Because it's all in the stretch before the release. In the words of the great tension-meister John Cougar Mellencamp: "It hurts so good."

Tension is also what makes stories especially powerful. The really good ones lead you to places and experiences you've never known, stretching and stressing you as far as you can go, before finally satisfying you with a fulfilling ending. A good joke does the same thing—it steers your brain one way as far as it can go, then punch-lines you back to fulfillment. The funny you feel comes out of that stretch.

Neuroscientist Dr. Paul Zak has conducted experiments showing that tension is an especially important mechanism to stimulate the release of oxytocin in our noggins. His team found that without the stressor of tension, the brain is actually stingy in its synthesis of neurochemicals. "When we showed these very flat stories with no tension," he said, "we saw the attention drop after about 20 seconds."

Incorporating tension, on the other hand, heightens attention because we have to feel ourselves released. We simply cannot leave or zone out mid-stretch.

Movies use tension religiously. Remember how the *Star Wars* story arc goes up and up, then eventually down? If we zoom in on that arc, we see that it's actually a series of waves. Going up, then down, then up, then down. Nearly every scene in *Star Wars* (or any movie) has tension built into it—drawing you in and letting you out, or throwing you around and setting you down.

In the words of the great tension-meister John Cougar Mellencamp: "It hurts so good."

Let's hear a pro describe it. Here's screenwriter Kevin Marburger:

> "Tension is a device writers use to keep audiences on the edge of their seats. We use it in comedy, drama, and of course, horror and thrillers. It's like throwing a bucket of ice on somebody. It wakes them up and keeps them engaged in the story."

Now let's hear from Kevin's writing partner, Michele Marburger:

> "The more you stretch them, the more they tense up. They're like a spring you pull, pull, pull, and then—bam!— you release the spring."

In fight scenes, tension is created and released in rapid succession. *Rocky* is a perfect example—we see Rocky on the ropes, and whenever a punch comes, we sway along with him, subconsciously avoiding the punch. Tension builds with the punch, then releases when we dodge it, but not completely released—we're still worried about getting knocked out. Then, when Rocky finally comes to life and starts turning the fight around, our excitement boils over—our arms might even make punching moves in sync with his, releasing all that tension we built up when we imagined being hit.

Tension can also touch us in a more sensitive way. You see this in romance movies; overtly in the "will they or won't they" plotlines, but also more subtly. Here's David Wiegand, Assistant Managing Editor and TV critic for the *San Francisco Chronicle* to talk about it:

> "Tension will make you want to know more and make you invest more in that scene, in that character … It doesn't nec-

Things humans love because of tension:

Drama

Sex

Sports

Games

Magic

Hot sauce

Yoga

Music

Jokes

Puzzles

The list goes on and on, but includes...

...Movies

3 KEYS TO ANTICIPATION:

1. Super intriguing setup

2. A hold that's long enough
   to create discomfort,
   but not so long that
   they grow tired

3. A payoff that's worth
   the wait

essarily have to be dramatic tension, like will he live or die. It can be emotional tension on different levels. It can be expectation and hope. Something you want to happen or being afraid that something may happen. Both are tension and pull viewers into the context."

So how do you, a manager or director at a corporation about to perform a presentation, use tension? Well, we actually mentioned a few ways in Chapter 6, like how I cut the lights before the big sales meeting, or how my workshop group hid the upticking number. Those are all about building tension, then—when the audience was right where we needed them—releasing it.

That movie you just saw is part of a presentation I give at conferences. I don't actually play the clip; I speak it and click the slides as I go. I use a few techniques to build tension, and as I perform it, I see people rise up in their seats while I stretch them. Let's now break down tension into some individual techniques you can use in your presentations, the way I used it in my example. There are four biggies: anticipation, pacing, framing, and music.

Anticipation

Let's start with anticipation since it's the tension technique we all know best. You heard me use anticipation in the tension clip when I told you I was going to share the "secret ingredient to everything we humans find interesting," but then... made you wait...a long time...so I could reel you into my net and finally reveal the answer as "tension."

What you felt was powerful, right? But anticipation has to be measured carefully and should be tested out with your objective editing team first to make sure you've got the timing right and don't wear people out. There are three main keys to crafting anticipation successfully:

1. The setup has to be super-intriguing and you must say it boldly.

2. Don't let the wait go too long or you'll lose them. Concentrate on the audience and you'll know when you've hit your limit and need to relieve the tension. For example, when I cut the lights back in that sales meeting in Chapter 6, I listened very hard to the audience until I started to hear some unrest. Then I listened even more intently, and when I heard it ramp up, that's when I hit the projector light to release it.

3. The "Aha!" has to be worth it. For instance, if I had just ended on the word "tension," I think you would have been disappointed. That's why I gave you more elaboration and performance. You had been through so much, you deserved it.

Pacing

Anticipation is actually part of pacing because pacing is the speed at which you deliver your information, and creating anticipation is just slowing everything down until we yearn for it. But pacing can be used in other ways as well.

In movies, pacing is mainly created through the speed at which the movie is cut. Fast cuts excite us, like action scenes and those ESPN promos. Long cuts relax us and allow us to take things in. Spending more time looking at a character also makes us feel like he/she is important. Check out how much longer George Clooney appears in each of his cuts as opposed to other actors. He usually plays heroic characters, so it's appropriate. Those long cuts help us feel that heroism.

You can use pacing when you're presenting by deciding the pace of your speech pattern. Speak slowly and you'll come across as thoughtful and authoritative, like a minister or a political candidate. Or if you want to get people excited, speak quickly, like a sportscaster.

It's also powerful to change it up in order to give people those peaks and valleys. For instance, in the tension clip you watched, I started speaking slowly to create anticipation; then, once I did my reveal with the word "tension," I went faster to wind everyone up again, going into overdrive when I reached the lines, "It's why we compete, wait till the last second, drive like maniacs."

But then...I slowed paused after the "and," to let everyone back down again with "it's why we learn our lessons when we do. It's all tension." I did that for two reasons: to give you a chance to relax, and to reset for the climax.

Movies use similar techniques when they edit. One of my favorites is called the "speed ramp." The editor

PLAY THE PACING EXAMPLE

You'll find it at www.gettotheheartbook.com/movies

In the movie above, we use pacing to bring a magnetic effect to two things most people find boring: quantitative data and housecleaning.

ramps up the speed of the footage to excite us, then slows it way down to make us focus on one specific thing. Done right, it feels like a magnetic force. Remember that iconic scene in *The Matrix* where Neo dodges the bullets? It's cut to be super fast, then out of nowhere, it slows down so you can see Neo's actual evasion movements. Do you remember how you reacted to that? I'll bet you were not only emotionally moved, but your body was probably trying to physically emulate his actions as well. Pacing, man: it's killer.

A close cousin to the speed ramp is the freeze-frame. In the middle of the action, the movement stops to make you concentrate on something. Freezing the movie in this manner also allows us to release our tension.

Speed ramps and freeze-frames work in corporate movies as well. To the left is a sample we quickly put together. To challenge ourselves, we made it about around two of the least sexy topics on the planet: quantitative insights and housecleaning. We used speed ramping, though, to make it engaging, but also to show how people feel throughout the process of cleaning their homes. Then we used freeze-framing to magnetically draw you in every time we wanted you to focus on a statistic. (Added bonus: it also gave me a way to con my friend Mia into cleaning my house.)

Framing

Framing is another tool movies use to create tension. It's not the framing of an argument, but more a synonym for "composition." It's the way things are placed on the screen. Framing wide so the hero is small will make you fear for him or her; framing close (like a George Clooney shot) will heighten your emotional attachment.

Framing is also a tool you can do with your body when you present. By choosing where you place yourself during your presentation, you can guide how you're perceived. If you want to be authoritative, stand back on a platform or stage that makes you taller. If you want to be more friendly or emotional, stand close to your stakeholders.

Movement accentuates both perceptions. In Hollywood, they move the camera on a stand with wheels called a "dolly." They dolly from one side to another to do that move-and-reveal shot we discussed back in Chapter 6, but dollying forward is probably the most powerful use. They call the shot a "dolly push," and you see it when-ever they want to make you feel more for a character. The camera begins moving toward the hero or the love scene, or whatever they want you to connect with, and that move-in for the close-up tightens the framing and engages your emotions. To the right, you'll see how they did it with Tom Hanks in *The Green Mile*. In the clip, Tom's character has to execute a man he knows is inno-cent. He has to keep a prison guard's face, but inside, he feels helpless; the director wants you to feel his anguish (and still like him), so they do a dolly push toward him to heighten your emotional bond.

PLAY THE FRAMING EXAMPLE

You'll find it at www.gettotheheartbook.com/movies

See how the camera getting closer to Tom Hanks makes you feel for him? You can do the same thing by slowly moving toward your stakeholders when you want them to emotionally connect with you.

If you want to stress a point with your audience, emulate the dolly push and slowly move closer as you speak.

They'll bond with you, just like they bond with the heroes they see in the movies.

You can emulate the dolly push with your feet. If you want to stress an emotional point and connect with your audience, move slowly toward them. Walking forward will have the same effect as a camera dollying in for a love scene. It will heighten the emotional connection your audience has for you. It will also increase the tension, making them listen even more intently. So when you finish your point and want to release it, simply move backward. It's all in the framing.

Music
Music is my favorite way to create tension because, as you heard in that tension clip, it's amazingly powerful. I think it's also the quickest, easiest way to set a mood and get people right into the place, time period, or style you want to create. It's as though it reaches right into your heart and gut. Joy, mystery, freedom, fear: all can be conjured up in a nanosecond with music and will last for a long, long time.

Who can forget the shark theme in *Jaws*? That built up so much tension in me that I was afraid to sit on a toilet for a month.

Composer Cody Westheimer has scored dozens of movies, so he knows how to wrap us around his finger. Here's how he uses music to build a climactic scene:

> "One of the things I love to do musically is to build, build, build. It might be at the climax of the entire film, then, at a strategic point, I stop: let the music go off the cliff … What that does to an audience is absolutely profound. It creates space for the big 'aha!' moment."

Music can also release the tension. A perfect example is the bus scene in *Almost Famous*. There's been fighting amongst the band, so everyone on the bus hates one another. It's tension upon tension upon tension. No music, just naked, awkward tension. Then Elton John's "Tiny Dancer" comes on the radio and everyone starts to notice. Some tap, others look around, then someone starts to sing. Then they all start singing and pretty soon, it's flowers, hugs, and unicorns. Yet it's feels authentic because of the music.

But back to you and your presentation

There are many kinds of music you can use to create and manage tension in your presentations and videos. Here are the big three:

Open music

Like its name, open music is perfect for opening a movie or presentation because it refreshes the room and welcomes people in. It feels fresh, like an ascending balloon or lemonade on a porch. If you play open music when people walk in and take their seats, your stakeholders will instantly relax and loosen up. To hear how it sounds, click on the speaker icon to the right that says "open music."

How did that make you feel? Light, airy? Any images come into your mind? That's how evocative music is.

Hold music

Music can also hold you in place. For instance, if you want to make people feel stressed, play one of those death-metal, troll-under-the-bridge songs, or some fast, free-form jazz (sorry, jazz fans, I'm a simple music guy). Either one will make people clench. Conversely, if you want to draw people in, give them something slower and embracing, like what you'll hear when you click on the speaker icon to the right that says "hold music."

Anybody sink into their seats? That's hold music.

A QUICK TASTE O' MUSIC

Hear an example of Open Music

(*Sondre Lerche's* To Be Surprised)

You'll find it at
www.gettotheheartbook.com/movies

Hear an example of Hold Music

(*Kate Bush's* This Woman's Work)

You'll find it at
www.gettotheheartbook.com/movies

THE POWER OF
PROPEL MUSIC

Play *the emotional shift that's driven by tension, led off with propel music. You'll find it at www.gettotheheartbook.com/movies*

There are definitely specific instruments that lend themselves to open and hold music. For instance, something about acoustic guitars really works for open music. Violins and breathy voices like Kate Bush lend themselves beautifully to an alluring kind of hold music.

Propel Music

When you want to excite your stakeholders or rally them on their way, music can also propel them forward. For that, let's bring back our friend Max. The clip I'm going to show you will actually use three of our tension techniques: framing, pacing, and music. Don't click on it yet, though—I want to tee it up for you.

The clip shows two opposite customer experiences. We'll start with Max's negative experience you saw earlier with the iPod and the car, back in Chapter 9. But then we're going to keep it rolling so you see it transition into a positive experience.

First, to make you feel Max's frustration, we're going to use hold music, as well as tight framing and slow pacing. Then we're going to swing into his positive experience and let Max have his day in the sun by opening up the framing, quickening the pace, and most importantly, switching from hold to propel music. To see it, click on the frame to the left or go to the URL below it.

Anybody shaking their groove thing? That's propel music, releasing your tension from the hold music and making you move. Did you feel the contrast between the two? Did you sense Max's emotional swing? That's tension and release.

Tension. It's a rollercoaster. It's a seduction. It's a twisted way to rule your audience's emotions. But like Mel Brooks said in *History of the World*: "It's good to be the king."

THE BIG TAKEAWAYS

from this chapter

Keynote-level speaking comes from dedicating yourself to performance, just like a comedian or a pop star.

Start by making two versions, so you can keep the one you perform live nice and lean. Aim for it to take no more than 50% of your allotted time.

Run your presentation by your elite, objective-editing team, listen to their feedback, and use it to make your presentation leaner and more powerful.

Rehearse your speech enough times to memorize it and own it, just like Beyoncé. Rehearse the opening at least 80 times so your mouth will work on its own until your nerves recover.

Get to know the room as early as you can, and if possible, use as much of your own equipment (computer, clicker) to minimize technical mishaps and stress.

All that prep is hard work, but the heavenly feeling you'll experience and the rock star adoration you'll receive will make it all worth it.

TENSION:

Human beings are addicted to tension, and your stakeholders are no different.

Pacing, framing, and music are your most powerful weapons. And you can emulate them with actions as easy as walking toward your stakeholders.

Anticipation can hold your audience in suspense and draw them in. The key is to hold it as long as they can stand it, but not so long that they grow tired.

Music is the elixir that never fails. There is music to open their minds, hold them in place, and propel them forward. A perfect opening song starts with either a slow build, easygoing pace, or an expansive sound.

CHAPTER 12

Success with Story

from two real-life strategic story directors

To make this thing completely real, I'd like to introduce you to two of my favorite clients: Catherine Lovazanno and Dave Decelle. Catherine and Dave have taken movie-style storytelling to heart and now use it every day to bring meaning and value to their companies, projects, and themselves.

But I'm going to shut up and let them tell you.

And now, Dave Decelle
Director Consumer Insights at Netflix:

At our October 2015 Quarterly Business Review meeting I had 20 minutes to tell the top 200 leaders at Netflix a story about our members' perceptions of our Netflix Originals strategy. This meeting is a pretty intense two days of information overload and vigorous debate. So I knew I had to tell a compelling, memorable story that would cut through the clutter.

In creating my story, I started with the climax: the point where all my plot lines come together to reveal the strategic opportunity, the risk of inaction and bad execution, and what success ultimately feels like to our members.

I then backed up and thought about the plot lines I would need to develop, the characters and their conflicts that would drive the story forward, and the moments of tension-and-release, tension-and-release that would keep my audience waiting to see what would happen next.

The plot lines were easy. They were essentially the "key takeaways" from a few research projects. I had a total of six of them, such as:

- While many people have heard of a certain show, far fewer realize that it is a Netflix Original.

- Connecting the Netflix brand name to a show can increase the appeal of that show.

Next came the moments of tension-and-release. This is by far my favorite storytelling technique! By building tension, people can't help but pay rapt attention to see what happens next. Here's one example. I took a certain Netflix original and showed the large percent of consumers who have simply heard of it. Then I showed the smaller percent who know they can watch it on Netflix, followed by the even smaller percent who know they can watch it only on Netflix, and ending with the smallest percent who know it is specifically a Netflix Original. The room got quieter and more still as I slowly revealed this downward trend. I could feel the tension build. Then, with the next slide, I released it: "The good news," I said, "is that all of these percentages have been increasing over the last year." Everyone was relieved and ready for the next part of the story. Because if you can keep your audience on this tension-and-release rollercoaster throughout your story, they can't help but pay attention to see what happens next. Think about it, have you ever seen anyone checking their email while riding a rollercoaster?

Next came character and conflict. I chose one of our originals to be a character in my story. So when I showed how awareness drops from "heard of show" to "know it's a Netflix Original," I showed an image of the main actor from the show getting smaller as the percentages shrank. Using an image of the main actor made it feel like a character in a story rather than an abstract bar on a chart. I also made Netflix and HBO characters in my story, with the conflict between them being consumers' differing perceptions of the two brands.

Driving my story forward at a good clip took a lot of work, but really paid off. This book makes the point that

> # "If you never turn away from your audience,
> ## they will never turn away from you."

humans have a shorter attention span than goldfish. Keeping that in mind, guess how many slides I created for this 20-minute story. 5? 10? Surely not more than 20, right? Wrong – I had 112 slides! Why? Because I told my story one point at a time, one point per slide, 10 seconds per slide. This increased focus and created story momentum. And my audience quickly realized that every 10 seconds they'd see something new on the screen, so if they checked even one email, they'd miss an important point. Again, I had them eagerly watching to see what would happen next.

Now to pull off 10-second slides it is extremely important to know your script and sync it with your transitions, animations and builds. Here's how I did it. After creating my 112 slides, I typed the 1-2 sentences I wanted to say in a light gray box at the bottom of each slide, with an asterisk at each point I needed to click. Then I practiced my script over and over by putting the deck in slideshow view and reading through my script at the bottom of each slide as I clicked along. By the time I got on stage I never once had to look over my shoulder to remind myself what's on screen and what I should say next. I've found that if you never turn away from your audience, they will never turn away from you.

I used several other tactics, but I'll give you just one more – make your audience part of the story. I did this in a very

simple way: I opened by asking the audience to raise their hand if they had heard of that certain Netflix original I mentioned earlier. Naturally everyone raised their hands, so I put "Netflix employees: 100% awareness" up on the screen. Then I showed them how consumer awareness levels drop off from "heard of show" to "know it's a Netflix Original." This made the point that inside the walls of Netflix everyone is hyper aware of every Netflix original, but real life is very different. My main point here is that by giving my audience even a bit-part in the story, they were more invested in its outcome from the very start.

Now let me tell you how my story ended. Through the rest of the two day meeting, people I had never met before gave me knowing smiles as they walked by or tipped their drink glasses to me from across the room to show their appreciation. I was invited by several VPs and Directors to come tell my story to their teams. And in his closing remarks, our CEO, Reed Hastings, stated that this was "the best consumer insights presentation yet."

I've since been asked to re-tell my story to at least eight teams across Netflix. Even months later, people sought me out and said, "My manager says you have a presentation about Netflix originals that I need to see."

That's the power of a great story, it makes a lasting impression and people want to share it with others.

And now, Catherine Lovazzano
UX and Design Research Lead at Fitbit

When you're deep in a project, it can often feel isolating, but when I was head of trends and foresight at FIAT Chrysler Automobiles, I was geographically isolated as well. My stakeholders were in Auburn Hills, MI and Solana Beach, CA; I was in San Francisco.

I flew a lot of miles to come see them, but I didn't always feel like my decks gave my stakeholders enough to truly understand or represent my work. I worried as well about how they might present it after I had to head back. Decks are so easily passed around, borrowed from, and repurposed, it's nearly impossible to keep the meaning behind your work intact.

I needed a different vehicle. One that would enable me to bring more of myself and the story to the table, that would be encapsulated so it could be passed around without losing integrity. One that would bring forward the emotions and the subtle nuances that give stakeholders the real and whole truth.

I had done video before, but this approach inspired a lot more confidence in me. It's more vivid, deeper, and at the same time, more concise. So I brought my decks over to Backstories and entered movie-style storyland.

This kind of storytelling requires getting things down to their essence, making choices early and thoughtfully, so we started by culling the decks down to the most powerful points. I loved the strategic aspect of it: framing the narrative but leaving space for exploration; anticipating the kinds of things we'd want to capture visually in field. It's a structure that lends itself to the kind of brevity and flow I knew would be appreciated at headquarters, and yet, it didn't feel constricting at all.

Filming our interviews was riveting. I knew how powerful video could be, but we captured so much more than I was used to. It wasn't just quotes, it was action and those moments that show the true spirit of consumers. Most importantly, we brought back the big "why" that you just can't do with stats and charts. And when a week or so later, I came back to see it all edited, I felt such pause and this huge rush of confidence. "We got it," I kept feeling. "We got it."

Presenting too was like night and day from before. With slides, it can be a battle to keep people engaged. When you play a video, though, it takes a lot of that pressure off. You don't have to be the only voice. You can be in the moment, feeling what your stakeholders feel, anticipating their questions, more consultative and strategic. And it's good that you are too because their questions tend to be so much deeper as well. It's like everyone steps up their game.

Probably the best example of the difference was a project we completed on the future of mobility. There were two phases, both presented to the highest level of management at FCA.

We gained clarity—a lot more clarity—and command, because when you tell stakeholders 50 things, you don't get to choose which five they remember.

Say five things, though, and you do.

We presented the first phase in 2012. But first we had to stare down the barrel of hundreds of pages of insights. We saw so many details, but no clear way to communicate what we knew was really exciting for FCA or the emotion that inspired us. So when we stepped up to present, we came off perfectly competent, but I have to admit, flat.

Fast forward to 2013, the design team had developed concepts from our work, so we now had compelling visuals for the end of our story, but we also knew expectations would be much, much higher. This time, though, we were going meet them, and then some.

So collaborating with Backstories, we honed our original 300-slide deck into a five-page story. Tightening this much was not easy by any stretch. It's many, many instances of "what am I going to give up?" vs. "what am I going to gain?" We gained clarity—a lot more clarity—and command, because when you tell stakeholders 50 things, you don't get to choose which five they remember. Say five things, though, and you do.

So this time, we brought a very different kind of presentation and a two-part video that took management through a cohesive, fluid story: an ambitious project that led to compelling insights, which then led to a sophisticated strategy, which then led to inspired, breakthrough designs. And that's exactly how FCA's top leadership saw it. They were so much more emotionally connected this time around. They finally saw what we saw and what made us so excited. They saw the "why" behind our insights and understood the decisions we made in our strategy. They were enthusiastic about the designs and felt so confident, they greenlit them for the next stage of development.

I cannot express how much more fulfilling this experience was. You really need to feel it on your own. But I can tell you that when I look at my past work, I'll sometimes see a deck and wonder why I did what I did. But that never happens with this kind of storytelling. Probably because so much forethought is built into process, the work still feels fresh, and is, without a doubt, the work I'm most proud of.

CHAPTER 13

The Goodbye Speech

Time to go out and start wowing

Ahhh, the last chapter. I hope this book inspired you, and you're already thinking about the projects you have on your desk and imagining the possibilities. And hopefully, like me, you're also enjoying a cocktail for all your hard reading.

To make it easier to start creating and building steam, I put together a website at gettotheheartbook.com. There you'll find a strategic map you can print out and blog entries covering topics that got axed by my elite team of objective editors (aka "baby killers")

It will also give you a place to ask questions and yap it up with people like you—your fellow Story Strategy Directors.

Fun fact: the last shot of a movie production is called the "Martini Shot."

I hope this book has also shown you how to use movie-style storytelling to change minds and build new ideas, and you're already thinking of ways to make your strategic presentations more interesting and exciting.

Here's a summary of the main takeaways:

Your *Get to the Heart* CliffsNotes in 15 bullet points:

1. Empathize with your audience, all their meetings, and all the crap they have to go through.

2. Ask yourself what they have to do with your information and what's needed for them to do it successfully.

3. Get a colleague outside your team to help you simplify your deck into just those core slides. Discard the rest or keep them in your hip pocket.

4. Make your information easier to understand by adding context in the form of characters, settings, and action.

5. Use "for example" to find those building blocks (characters, settings, action).

6. Use "so" to frame it in your stakeholders' context—give them a way to put your ideas into action.

7. Once you've got the simple story down, find ways to show it visually. Look on stock sites, but don't be afraid to shoot photos on your own. It's often quicker and gives you more of what you need.

8. When you need to be more than just clear, remember: the rational mind steers, but emotion is what really moves people. Together, they make for a one-three punch.

9. Put together a compelling opening—let your stakeholders know this won't be the same old bore-fest.

10. Show them heroes that can bring your information to life and make it more personal and affecting.

11. Don't just tell your information—*show* it with action.

12. Build a cause to provide clarity and desire, and really get buy-in.

13. Prepare your presentation like a keynote would. Rehearse, rehearse, rehearse until your mouth can move on its own and you can look your audience straight in their eyes.

14. Use tension to guide their emotions, hearts, and gut.

15. Have yourself a cocktail.

These 15 keys can be applied to any project: large, small, qualitative, quantitative, strategy, marketing, corporate communications, sales, expensive, cheap, even quick-turnaround projects. Anything can be storified like a movie, and when it is, be prepared to go farther than you ever have before.

Your *Get to the Heart* CliffsNotes in story form
You don't have to be like everybody else. You can make a bigger difference for your stakeholders, colleagues, and customers by presenting stories instead of blasting everyone with information. You can do it by taking cues from the ways movies tell their stories.

First, empathize with what your audience goes through so you can provide that glass of water they're thirsting for, connect with them more deeply, and find your work more fulfilling.

You'll ask yourself more about what your stakeholders need to accomplish, and then, what information you have that will help them do it right (and what won't). And finally, you'll ask yourself what style of presentation or takeaway will be easiest and most enjoyable for them to learn from you.

Using those answers as a guide, you'll simplify your information. You'll get friends and colleagues to act as a sounding board and you'll kill any parts that don't further your presentation's story or its meaning.

Then you'll find the characters, settings, action, and theme that will bring your information to life.

Once you get your story down, you'll make it visual so everyone can see what you see. You'll use both stock images and shoot your own so you can make it even more clear.

When that big presentation rolls around, you'll speak to your stakeholders' elephants as well as their rational minds and deliver the passion that ignites them, the understanding that leads them in the right directions, and the confidence that will sustain them.

As you craft your story, you'll follow the map to get your stakeholders out of the conference room and into the world of your insights and ideas. You'll then evoke urgency and credibility, and through your heroes and the visual simplicity of seeing them in action, you'll recruit your audience into your revolution with a compelling, rallying cause.

And because you prepared so well and put on a tension-filled performance, you'll feel amazing and everyone will look at you like you're made of gold.

Then, as you bid them adieu, they'll walk out energized and ready to inspire others with their own clarity about what needs to be done and their desire to make it happen. They'll value your recommendations, and put them into action.

Your stakeholders and their colleagues will request you for their most important projects, and you'll soon see your ideas end up in the marketplace—where you can see them, your spouse can see them, your friends can see them, and even your mom can see them. Where they truly, truly belong.

Eventually, you'll earn a seat at the big table. And your ideas, insights, and visions will never, ever, ever, ever end up in that filing cabinet we call the morgue.

Making this kind of difference may seem idealistic, but I've seen these techniques succeed for nearly every client I've worked with. You heard firsthand the stories from Dave and Catherine. At first, it's a bit more work, but then as the rewards make you more committed, big things will happen for you.

Truth is, you're probably already putting in the time and sweat just doing what you're doing. So you might as well look sexy doing it, right?

My final goodbye—sort of

Before I send you off, I want you to know that I've also added some bonus features on the next 30 or so pages:

- What you can do if you only have one hour, one day, or one month to prepare a presentation.

- A list of the projects that benefit most from videos and movie-style storytelling

- How to film interviews and action, what gear to buy or rent, and some stock footage and music sites.

- How to get the most out of professional videographers and editors.

Oh, and one last thing: I encourage you to ask me any questions that arise when you're bringing movie-style storytelling to the conference room.

I want you to succeed—big time—so fire away and I'll try to get back to you within a few days. Just go to *www.gettotheheartbook.com* and ask for Ted.

Okay, crew, that's a wrap.

Bonus Features

Some practical ways to use your new wisdom

I want to make this book as helpful as possible—right now—so I'm including information you can use today. On the next few pages, you'll find articles on what you can do within the constraints of different deadlines: from one hour to a month or more.

Then, in an effort to be helpful in a gazillion ways, I've added a series of articles you may not need today, but could be useful in the near future, including which projects I've seen benefit from movie-style storytelling and a how-to on making the actual videos, both on your own and with professionals. I hope you get a ton of information, skills, and confidence from them.

What To Do If You Only Have ...

...ONE HOUR

Pick the most important point you want to make, then give it a context that helps your stakeholders understand the information and how they can use it.

You can do it in three steps:

1. Look for the characters, setting, and plot. Take your chart, data, or point you want to make and study it again until you know exactly what it's about. Then say the words "for example," and see what pops into your head. It will probably be the makings of a very simple story. Put it on paper or your screen and refine it a bit until you feel good about its ability to make your point clearly.

2. Now take it one step further. Think of your stakeholders and what they'll get out of your point, then say your story aloud again and add the word "so" at the end. Again, see what pops into your head. It may not come easy the first time, but it will soon. And you'll have a very clear way to understand your point, and the value in it.

3. When your story is complete, find a photo or illustration that helps people visualize it. Then build your slide, one piece of information at a time, like I did with Puppy Claus.

If you finish all that in under an hour, do it again with the second most important point.

...ONE DAY

Do the same thing you did above with "for example" and "so," but expand it to your three most important points.

Then take the steps to understand your stakeholders and simplify your presentation. Ask yourself the two key questions that allow you to empathize with your stakeholders and frame your information in the way that gets you heard:

What do they need to do with the information?

What, within all your slides, is the only information they'll need to do that thing successfully?

Then start simplifying. Grab a colleague and tell them what you want your stakeholders to get out of your presentation, then let them kill your babies. Remember: you don't want six hundred words; you want "Hard Rock, Rock Hard."

...ONE WEEK

Do the same thing as above, but take it further by tying your points into an overarching story, using the story-flow map. Tailor your story to their natural learning style and really incorporate it, especially with your opening and cause sections. Challenge yourself to come up with something truly refreshing and relevant for your stakeholders. Feel free to have someone else help you.

And rehearse, rehearse, rehearse—until you know it so well, you no longer have to look at the big screen behind you, just the laptop in front of you. Rehearsing will help you relax enough to appear loose and confident when you're presenting. Then rehearse your opening even more until you can say it in your sleep. That way, even if you get nervous, your mouth will save you.

...ONE MONTH

Do the same as above, but add visuals so your story has action, the way I did with the Millennials credit card series in Chapter 3. If you can find perfect visuals on a stock photo site, great. Otherwise, shoot the photos yourself or hire a photographer.

...MORE THAN A MONTH

More than a month? Chances are you have a high-stakes presentation on your hands. If I were you, I'd knock it out of the park by including a movie with your presentation, then craft different variations of it for each of your stakeholders like we did in the medical-device case history back in Chapter 4. Shameless plug: Backstories Studio can put the movies together for you, start to finish.

Then, here's how I would roll my presentation. I would open with the movie. That will immediately get your stakeholders into your story. Then, as you go through your presentation, use clips from the movie as they apply to your slides. That will reinforce your message, give you a throughline that keeps it tied together, and allow for breaks so you don't have to be the entire show. At the end, I would give everyone a copy of the movie to take with them.

While it may seem repetitive, it won't be when you're experiencing it for the first time like your stakeholders are. Because you're not playing the movie, then playing it again in the same form. In the second showing, it's parsed out so it feels different, and reinforces your message. When our clients present with this strategy, they've told me that the level of questions they get at the end is far deeper; they can tell stakeholders are truly engaged and already thinking about how they can use the information.

Departments and projects that can benefit from the power of a movie

At this point, you may be looking at the projects on your desk and thinking, "Which of these should I turn into a movie?"

As I hinted in the last chapter, not every project is a good fit for movies. If the message is "Consumers prefer this color blue" or "Building our garage here costs less and holds more cars," a movie is not worth the effort or expense. Save your budget until you have something that requires movie value.

On that subject, I'd like to share the wisdom of my longtime friend and colleague, Kevin Waters, managing director at Incite. The exec team at his former company instructed their managers to present in a manner that was this brief:

1. Remind stakeholders of the business question you've come to answer.

2. Tell them the answer.

3. End of story.

So what kinds of projects would benefit from movies and movie-style storytelling? Projects that need to persuade or inspire, like when you have to rally the whole company around a central mission, strategy, or sense of purpose, or a high-stakes project that requires buy-in. Those projects are well worth a movie because the ROI is so high. In fact, as discussed earlier, when your message goes out to all your company's employees, movies can actually be your most cost-effective option. When we did a segmentation project for an auto company, it went out to 10,000 employees. That brought down the cost of each four-minute movie to $1.45 per employee.

One thing to keep in mind: the project doesn't have to be current. If you're sitting on information that would still benefit your company, you can add new value by pulling it out of the cabinet and updating it with the movie treatment.

Here's my list of projects that can benefit appreciably from movie-style storytelling and how movie stories can help your cause, your influence, and ultimately, your career. Maybe you've got one of these projects on your desk right now. (Even if you don't, this list will prepare you for future movie projects.)

Short list of potential movie projects

First up is the short list. Each company is different, so I've listed projects under the most common fiefdoms (and sometimes under more than one). There's also a long list below, with explanations on how movies can increase the project's impact and value. Because the list is broken down by department, feel free to skip the ones that don't apply to you.

Consumer Insights

- Segmentation
- Personas
- Customer experience
- Patient journeys
- Paths to purchase
- Bad news (never deliver this yourself)
- Analytics
- Perception

Strategy

- Futures scenarios
- Competitive landscape maps
- Strategic models
- Sales funnels
- C-level presentations
- Ideation stimuli (inspirational materials)
- Strategic rollouts

Marketing

- Positioning
- Brand frameworks
- Sales funnels
- Company stories
- Website movies for products and product features

Sales

- Sales funnels
- Key account presentations
- Pitch meetings/capabilities presentations
- Constituent presentations (franchisees, bottlers, dealers, etc.)
- Rep bios
- Annual sales meetings
- Global sales force synergy

Human Resources & Corporate Communications

- Recruitment
- Onboarding
- New policies
- Department profiles
- Employee synergy
- Founder/heritage stories
- Employee loyalty
- Teamwork initiatives
- Philanthropy

Operations

- Store-level communications

Training & Development

- Onboarding
- Presentation training
- Any other training that wouldn't be ruined by lawyers

Creative/Design

- Inspiration from insight & strategy briefs
- Presentations to C-suite

And now, the long list

Again, feel free to skip to your department and/or the areas that impact you. Or if you want to school another department that bores you on a regular basis, check out their list and together we'll make them step up their game.

(If you do read more than one department's list, you may see some repetition. Sorry about that; I'm just trying to take care of the single-department folks.)

Consumer Insights

Segmentation

Segmentations can be difficult for colleagues to get their heads around, yet they're the building blocks of marketing and the core of a company's success. Movies can bring each segment to life, allowing employees and stakeholders to deeply understand and empathize with each segment. They are especially useful after the segmentation is quantified and validated—the movie doesn't have to do the validation itself, it only has to present the data in a relatable and memorable way, with inspirational heroes whom everyone can understand and feel for. If you want to show a side-by-side comparison of the segments, the movies are best accompanied by a poster.

Personas

Speaking of heroes: personas are absolutely meant for movies. Just like with segmentations, you can bring them to life and rally everyone to create and problem-solve around a likeable protagonist that you could name "Sara." A character like Sara is more powerful and inspiring than "Heavy Users."

Customer experience

Movies portray the customer experience in ways that no other form can. Your audience doesn't have to read it or hear the experience—they can see and feel it. If you're a stakeholder in charge of crafting that experience, it's amazing how many ideas you'll come up with when you feel what the customer feels. Movies are also effective with customer experience maps. The map provides the visual path of the experience, while the movie can show the brand cues, how customers react and interact with them, and how they shape customer emotions and perceptions. So everyone can see how consumers respond, engage, choose, and behave.

Patient journeys

Like showing customer experience, patient journey movies help pharmaceutical stakeholders understand what patients go through at each step—where they encounter the anxiety that can emotionally paralyze them, where there are opportunities to relieve that stress, and which players (doctors, support staff, caregivers) are influential. This allows pharma companies to help patients adhere to their treatment protocols, and ultimately get better—results that are important to the company. Patient journey movies work best when they bring to life a map of the entire process, presented on a poster where stakeholders can see the whole journey and ideate around it.

Paths to purchase

Similar to patient journeys, movies bring the emotional "why" to a map's "who," what," and "where."

Bad news

I once had a project where consumers said the product reminded them of dog food. It was horrible news, but it spoke to the heart of what was holding back the product, so I had to say it in my presentation. I learned a lesson that day: the bearer of bad news never gets a fair trial. So if you have to deliver consumer feedback you know will be controversial, I highly suggest you film the consumers saying it, then let them speak for themselves so they're the messengers, not you. You'll be astonished how attentive your stakeholders will be; it might be depressing to realize that the opinions of anonymous consumers have more sway than you, but it's worth it when you can present a clear, honest message.

Analytics

Analytics are perfect tools for showing us the "what, "where," and "how," but have a hard time showing the "why." That's where movies come in: they bolster sophisticated data by portraying people in real-life scenarios and showing emotions that base the analysis in a human context, lending the data even more credibility.

Perception

What people say about brands and products is only part of the story. True understanding comes from seeing their faces, hearing the expression in their voices, sensing their energy. That's when you get a much better idea of what they really think. Movies are the only way you can get to those nuances (short of in-person observation, but we know how much that method costs).

Strategy

Futures scenarios

These took off in a big way with a movie from Royal Dutch Shell: they created multiple hypothetical futures about energy and how people might shape their lives around each one. Movies can zoom in on those scenarios by showing them at the customer level. For instance, a movie persona can show you what that persona's attitudes and behaviors might be in each future possibility you map out. This makes the scenario more relatable, inspiring employees to be empathic and formulate more viable ideas.

Competitive landscape maps

A movie cannot replace a map itself, but it can add an urgency that makes stakeholders want to capitalize on its opportunities. It can also build credibility by showing competitors in action, as well as showing your consumers talking about the perceptions that often inform those maps.

Strategic models

Even a well-executed strategic model is hard to grasp without someone presenting it—each is unique and complex. But if you're the CEO, you want people to understand and use them. Movies can bring strategic models to life in a truly human way. It still helps to be there in person to answer questions, but it may no longer be necessary. Your stakeholders will not only get it, they'll get behind it.

Sales funnels

Similar to a path to purchase, a movie accompanying a poster or graphic slide will provide the "why" customers do what they do and choose what they choose, as well as consumer perceptions—of you and your competitors—each step of the way.

C-level presentations

Once you've ideated on each future and have your competitive landscape map, a strategic model, and a sales funnel, it's time to present to the execs. You have ninety minutes and an absolute ton of information. What you also have, but might not be aware of, is a storyline perfect for a movie or a series of movies. Nothing opens up execs to your ideas or supports your presentation better than your good friend cinema. Movies allow execs to see your logic and "sense the sense," and they'll have no choice but to run with it. Every time our clients used movies to open their presentations and reinforce their message throughout, they've hit home runs.

Ideation stimuli

With all those department-head salaries going offsite, ideation is one of the most costly activities for any business. But you do it because you need ideas, and executive contribution helps you get more buy-in. We all know how painful and humiliating it is to be short on ideas or to have your ideas received unenthusiastically. The key to coming up with good ideas by the dozen is stimuli that help you and the execs visualize and empathize. Movies do that so well. Instead of ideating on a consumer segment like "enhancers," you can bring enhancers to life by showing a real customer in the exact situations you're ideating to solve. When you and your colleagues can ideate around "Monica" (or whatever you name your poster child) and her situations, I'd bet the farm you'll be at least 30 percent more productive and 50 percent more of your ideas will be "on target."

Strategic rollouts

With the C-suite on board, it's time to get the departments to buy into your strategies so they'll get adopted and flow into innovation. You can show each department and stakeholder a similar version of the movie you showed to execs, with one key difference: get footage of those execs endorsing your strategy. Your colleagues will fall right in line.

Marketing

Positioning

Getting colleagues and stakeholders to understand your brand's positioning can sometimes be a walk in the park; unfortunately, more often it's a challenge. Recently, we did a positioning strategy for a luxury carmaker. Luxury is a positioning unto itself, but with 10 or so brands competing in that space, they're all looking for their place inside that luxury positioning. You can imagine how hard it is to differentiate yourself. And teaching your teams and outside stakeholders like ad agencies about the difference between you and Lexus is one tough teach. Movies can help you express the nuances that make your brand unique, and give you a chance to show customer testimony that reinforces your positioning strategy.

Brand frameworks (also called "essence")

I come from advertising, and it's all about brevity. That's why ad headlines are so succinct. And yet the average brand framework deck I've seen is 50 slides. Movies can help you shorten that education process and give the creatives your brand framework in a way that works for them: visuals, emotion, action, drama, and music. When when we do brand frameworks at Backstories, we actually take that approach one step further by designing our video in the same form that ad agencies use themselves: the rip-o-matic.

Company stories

More and more websites are featuring company-story movies on their home pages, and for good reason: visitors now expect them. And why not? They're a much easier experience. The key is presenting a real movie that tells your company's story, positioning, and key messages in a way that will resonate, with a voice that evokes trust and confidence. That's so much more persuasive than a simple video tour. They're also amazingly effective at opening capabilities presentations. Start your presentation with a movie and your customers will already know you, trust you, and open up themselves—which is exactly what you want.

Website movies for products and features

With the trend of companies presenting their product or website features in video form, you can't be behind the curve. Like company stories on your website, movies can help you leapfrog your competitors. Most of your competitors are developing "explainer" videos that primarily use animation to show how the feature works. Certainly appropriate in some cases, but most of the time, movies are more effective because they go beyond merely explaining.

If you're about to do a movie on your new product or feature, there's a reason you developed or improved it: you wanted to enhance the customer experience. That new element will have a real-life story where the change actually improves someone's life. Is that not a story made for a movie? Example: we're about to make one for an online retailer who developed a feature that alerts consumers when their "wish list" item goes on sale or to a price they set beforehand. It's super easy to explain, and the company could have simply done an explainer video.

Instead, we created a scenario showing how this would benefit the consumer: the ability to buy something indulgent. Many of us play this game in our heads when we want something but we can't justify the price. As kids, we knew we'd have to get it past our parents, and as adults, we have to get it past our own budget (or even scarier, our spouse). In this scenario, we created a consumer who had always pined for a Fender Telecaster guitar. But being a practical husband and father, he knew it was a luxury item and not justifiable.

Enter our retailer and their alert system, which allows him to set a price when the guitar enters the "what the hell" range. There's lots of fast, exciting shots of him interacting with the website, then a little anticipation, and finally, a victory shot of him striking a Pete Townshend power-chord jump—enhanced by a loud, sustaining rock 'n' roll guitar chord that drives the point home. It's also a little out of tune to make it more human. You can see this "victory pose" to the left.

In other words, the feature is explained, but in a way that captivates you and makes you wistfully ponder all the things on <u>your</u> wish list.

Sales funnels

Similar to a path to purchase, a movie accompanying a poster or graphic slide will provide the "why" customers do what they do and choose what they choose, as well as their perceptions of you and your competitors at each step. We did one for a car company that involved mounting iPads on a big poster, featuring short movies for each step of the funnel. It gave the funnel much more context, making it easier to understand and believe.

Sales

Key account presentations

The same way presenting to the C-level execs is high stakes for an internal department, presenting to a key account can mean even more

Explainer videos aren't just about the features. You can show the story of how that feature brings emotional value to your customers.

pressure for a sales team. If you're losing shelf space at Home Depot, it can absolutely kill your year. You do not want to lose that fight by bringing their buyers a boring PowerPoint deck. A movie can show a key account like Home Depot how your customers are *their* customers and how they want this partnership to work. It's a far more convincing way to persuade your key accounts. And you don't have to grovel.

Pitch meetings/capabilities presentations

Imagine you're in a meeting where some company is pitching you on a product or service. Chances are you've been corralled by a colleague and aren't even sure why you've been invited. Now imagine you're the sales team pitching at that meeting. Talk about a harsh environment, especially at the beginning. Starting off with a movie can take that pressure off you, warm up your prospects, and simplify your sell.

Constituent presentations
(franchisees, bottlers, dealers, etc.)

If you're Coca-Cola, you have bottlers. If you're Wing Stop, you have franchisees. If you're Toyota, you have dealers. All are key customers that, unlike key accounts, actually band together into associations with massive power. If you deal with them, you know what kind of power I'm talking about. You also know that sometimes they're not nice about it. They're often suspicious of corporate initiatives and don't like being told what to do. Not unlike a pitch meeting, a movie can warm them up and explain a new initiative or campaign in a way that makes sense and conveys the potential for success.

I also like to flip the traditional customer experience presentation that reports consumer feedback. The ones I've seen are filled with consumers complaining. If you were a car dealership group watching corporate give this kind of presentation, would you want to listen? I probably wouldn't; in fact, I'd feel like flipping them the bird. What's more effective and unifying is to interview the most successful franchisees, bottlers, etc., and get to the same information but in a positive way—from the people constituents trust and want to emulate. If they see successful people like themselves talking about how they earn their customers' trust, overcome buyer anxiety, or get them excited about their new purchase, it's the same message outcome as consumers complaining about what they're not getting. In fact, it's even more powerful because it's a 180° attitude adjustment—a way that resonates and inspires because you've made heroes out of their own people. Adding a label across the screen with each hero's dollar volume doesn't hurt either.

Rep bios

How many bios have you read that mention credentials, areas of expertise, and love of cooking, travel, and dogs? Blah, blah, blah, boring, boring, boring. With a movie, you skip all that vanilla and give your prospects a bio that will earn their trust. An expression of your passion and expertise in a way that's relevant, like the satisfaction you derive from fulfilling a client's need—and anticipating that need can show who you are in a way that prospects care about. They see you know your stuff, and their needs are right in your wheelhouse. The care they see in your face and hear in your voice evokes trust and confidence. It's far more persuasive than a typical bio, and way more sexy. And you can get all that across in about a minute, so it can be delivered right into their email inbox.

Annual sales meetings

Oh yeah, all that fun in Vegas. All those sales reps having a great time, and the company spending gazillions to make sure they do. A series of movies can make sure the company gets the most out of their investment by guiding the emotions of reps throughout the meeting.

Back in Chapter 6, I told you about how we zapped all the sales reps into the same headspace to open the meeting with a bang. Here's how you can use movies throughout the day to keep everyone engaged and in the head and heartspace that helps them and the company get the most out of the day.

As the meeting progresses, you can use movies to break up the monotony of podium lectures and set up the reps for the mood that will help them succeed. When you want them to ideate, play an inspirational movie. When you want them to bond, show something funny that stars their colleagues, like a spoofy version of a famous music video. When you want them to be moved, play a movie that renews their sense of purpose. And when you want them to leave with a huge desire to kick ass, rally them with a confidence movie about an audacious goal.

Global sales force synergy

Large companies—and sometimes smaller ones—have reps all over the world, and even with those expensive annual sales meetings, companies still have to get everyone on the same page when they're not in Vegas. Movies are an effortless way to accomplish that. They can also be edited for email or watched on a phone without Wi-Fi. In these situations, we often divide long stories into one-minute episodes, so our clients can keep up the momentum and reps can absorb the episodes one at a time.

Sales funnels

Sometimes the sales department will put together a sales funnel showing the company how customers really buy. Again, a movie accompanying a poster or graphic slide will provide the "why" customers do what they do and choose what they choose and also sheds light on their perceptions of you and your competitors at each step. We did one for a car company where we mounted iPads on a big poster, featuring short movies for each step of the funnel. It gave the funnel deeper context, making it much easier for marketing to understand and believe in the strategy.

Human Resources and Corporate Communications

Recruitment

Your specific industry will determine whether you need to court employees. A movie that conveys that your company is strategic, sophisticated, and headed for bigger things can be quite persuasive, even more than money (but maybe not more than free sodas). It also doesn't hurt to show how fun your employees are, but even more persuasive is your people coming across as colleagues your prospects can look up to. Finally, you can often leverage a lot of the content from your existing company-story movie. It's amazing how simply changing music to something youthful can add the fresh energy that "the kids" are expecting right now.

Onboarding

Do you remember the last time you started a new job? Were you handed fifteen decks about the company and asked to read them? Once you read them, were you still completely lost at your first meetings? Did you feel small, or like you just wanted to shout, "I swear, you guys, I'm smart!" If so, you're not alone; most people have told me that's how it feels. And I know you're smart—it's just that fifteen decks in the first month of a job is overwhelming for anyone; it's too much, too soon. What if, instead of fifteen decks, you were shown a five-minute movie with your company's story and how your department fits in? If you're in marketing, it could be a profile of key customers, your company's positioning, and how it's different than your competitors. If you're in sales, it could be about the ideal clients, their needs, and the value your company brings them. Seriously, that can all be covered in five minutes—easy. And new hires will be excited, retain more, and start contributing right away.

New policies

Have you noticed that most new things in life are viewed with a little suspicion? That's certainly true with a new policy. Unless it's about raises or more vacation, people are going to wonder what the real motivation is. In other words, it's going to get emotional real fast. A movie can shift that anxiety 180°. Even if it's just a big-wig explaining the new policy with some passion, you can infuse the trust you need for the policy to be adopted wholeheartedly and keep the drama to a minimum.

Department profiles

I've been to many ideation meetings where department heads had no idea what other departments actually did. I was at one where the directors didn't know that some of the other departments even existed. It's called "silos," and it's amazingly common. And that's at the director level, where they regularly go to central meetings. Now think about it on the department level, where employees have virtually no exposure to other departments at all. So what if every department produced its own one-minute movie that took you through what they did and how they contributed to the company's overall goals? What if the movie also made them look like heroes? The companywide goodwill generated would be fantastic, producing more inspiration, more synergy, and more camaraderie.

Employee synergy

Because movies are a more universal and concrete experience than nearly any other media tool, they're a powerful way to get everyone on the same page. Remember how if you put the word "fish" up, everyone has a different picture, but if I play a video of a fish, we have a more common understanding? When you have a companywide message, being this clear is especially effective. Whether you have 100 or 10,000 employees, it's much easier to manage that group when everyone is unified with a single vision. So next time, roll the cameras and watch it bring everyone together.

Founder/heritage stories

Many companies have a rich history, and it's often beneficial to employees to learn more about it, especially if the founders are still alive. Employees will relate to the founder's struggle, how they kept their dream focused, and how happy they are to see people striving for that same dream today. A company heritage movie makes the founders feel honored, as they deserve to be. And just like your grandparents, they have a lot to say.

Employee loyalty

I'm sure you've cried while watching a movie, and I know you've laughed. I'll bet there were even times when you came out of a movie with a new sense of excitement or hope, then later connected and shared your feelings with others who saw the same movie. See where I'm going here? Movies are unparalleled in their ability to bring people together around a sense of purpose. A pharmaceutical company profiles a man whose life was saved by one of their medications. A mother shows us how something as mundane as a cleaning product allows her to be a laid-back mom who doesn't worry about spills on the coffee table, so her kids can play with impunity, and she can feel the joy of motherhood—all because of a cleaning spray. Yay cleaning spray! Movies excel at showing team members how

their company makes a difference for customers, and how they're a part of that difference.

Philanthropy

Talk about good feelings. When a company throws a philanthropic event like painting a school or cleaning a beach, it can bring the entire organization together. Producing a movie about such an event can take everyone right back to that warm and fuzzy camaraderie, making employees proud, department heads smile, and the PR department weep tears of joy.

Operations

Store-level communications

I've never run an enterprise with employees all over the world, or even around the country, but I imagine it's quite a wild beast. Wouldn't a tool that communicates the "how, what, where, and why" of your initiative make it more manageable and successful? With movies, you can send everyone the same message in a form your people can easily see, hear, and feel, so they're all on the same page.

Training & Development

Onboarding

On their first day, employees are handed fifteen decks about the company and asked to read them. Most feel lost and some are afraid they'll appear stupid. What if instead of fifteen decks, you showed them a five-minute movie of your company's story and how their department fits in? You could also include the company's commitment to training and the various courses employees are encouraged to take. You could have employees talking about the payoff they got from their training.

Presentation training

If your company can't do movies, you can still bring movie-style storytelling to your presentations. Sorry to plug myself, but we do a workshop that specifically covers movie-style storytelling for presentations.

Any training that wouldn't be ruined by lawyers

I have no idea how much the legal department directs the acting and final production of training videos, but I do know that most people laugh at them. Unfortunately, not in a good way.

The funny thing is that we've seen training films that are engaging and inspiring, like cooking shows and even infomercials. ESPN sometimes posts the NHL safety videos when they need to explain a referee call or why a player was suspended. They use cinematic techniques like close-ups to make them more concrete and believable. And it works.

Creative/Design/Development

Creative briefs

Briefs for the creative and design departments aren't actually generated by them, but they're the key tools that other departments (often insights and strategy) give them or their agencies to inform and inspire them. Unfortunately, they're rarely inspiring, and they're certainly not brief. They should be simple and visual because that's what creatives and designers need to stimulate ideas. And they should be filled with emotion. That's what sparks creative. If you can translate your brief into a movie that's simple, visual, and visceral, you'll end up with creative and design work that's more impactful and on target.

Presentations to C-suite

The opposite scenario is also tough for creative departments as well as product developers. When a big new product, ad campaign, or product line needs approval, it usually has to get the green light from the head honchos. So these departments have to make a business case for their work that the honchos can understand and believe in.

Today's creatives, developers, and designers seem to know more than I did back in the day, and they're certainly more aware of data and strategy. But if you're one of them, aren't you still scared to death about making that business case to the execs? When it's time to tell the story of how your work was inspired by the insights, vision, and strategy described in your brief, a movie is the most compelling way to show it. Imagine showing the insights through footage of consumers, then the opportunities through animation, then ramping the music to introduce the strategy that capitalizes on those opportunities. And then, how all this information inspired the minds of your team—projecting you as the heroes that created the amazing ideas and solutions that made the company rich and sexy.

When You're Up for Making a Movie

Gear it up

Are you as excited as I was when I first got into making movies? Awesome—you've got a kickass hobby ahead of you. There's so much to learn and enjoy, and movies offer the greatest feature any hobby can have: gear. Lots and lots of fascinating, cool-looking, technowonderful, and (my favorite part) occasionally expensive gear.

That said, it's really easy to get sucked into buying gear you won't need. I bought a mini-Steadicam because it was so magical, then I found out it takes an hour to set up. So guess how often I use it? Wait until you have a couple of movies under your belt, then you'll know what's required.

This recommendations list represents a sweet spot between "high quality" and "easy to use." It isn't the cheapest you can find, but it will get you a level above the Black Friday gear. Most of the items aren't professional grade for a reason: the more professional a camera is, the fussier it gets. That's perfect for people who use them regularly, but difficult when you don't. Here's what I like for the part-time movie mogul. (Note: All prices reflect the Spring 2016 market.)

What to buy at the camera store

It's always tempting to buy everything online, but some things, like cameras, have to be tried out in person. A real camera store (not a Best Buy) is also a great place to ask questions and learn. And it doesn't cost any more than Amazon. All cameras have standard pricing.

GEAR TO START WITH

Canon Vixia G20	*Sennheiser EW100*	*Tripod*	*Camera Bag*

Canon Vixia HF G20 – $750

It's full HD and automatic everything—you can open it up and have a good-looking picture in seconds. It comes with both an SD memory card and its own internal memory. I prefer using the SD card—you're not stuck worrying about your camera filling up with footage you're afraid to erase. It also has an external microphone jack. This is absolutely critical, because high quality audio is even more important than a high quality picture. (We'll discuss audio in a bit.) Finally, it has a "hot shoe" mount on top so you can easily hold our next item, which is…

Sennheiser EW100 Wireless Lavalier Mic – $630

This mic sounds phenomenal. It's wireless so your interviewees can move around and turn their heads without their voice dropping out because they're no longer facing the mic. They'll also feel like they're on a talk show. And it's built like a tank. Mine's been dropped at least 100 times and still works great.

Tripod – about $200

Another thing that seems okay to buy online—but don't. You have to feel it and work with it to know if a tripod will work *for* you. The wrong gear can work *against* you, distract you from doing your best work, and of course, become a huge pain the butt.

Get a tripod that's lightweight, but not too light. You don't want it blowing over in a breeze. For the same reason, get one that *feels* solid too.

Make sure it's easily adjustable. Again, you'll end up hating it if it's not. Get one with a fluid head so you can pan and tilt while you film. And make sure it's got a quick release so it's easy to pull on and off.

Camera Bag – about $50

It's easy to think you don't need to go to the camera store for something as simple as a bag, but you want it to feel like it was made for your gear. The

---

Wasabi Batteries

SanDisk SD Cards

Ultimate Lithium Batteries

LaCie Rugged Hard Drive

best way to do that is to bring all your gear to the store and see how it all fits.

Get a bag that fits everything you need, but also has extra space. It's inevitable—once you get into moviemaking, you'll want more stuff. Make sure it has small pockets for accessories, a shoulder strap, and plenty of padding in case you drop it, which you will (I drop mine about three times a year).

What to buy online
Small things like accessories are much cheaper online and worth buying there.

Wasabi Batteries – $22
These batteries work almost as well as Canon batteries for a third of the price. Get a package that also includes a car charger and wall charger. They're only a few dollars more.

SanDisk 16GB SD cards – $8.50
It holds three-plus hours of footage. Get Class 10. They're fast and reliable. Also, get yourself a case that holds at least twelve cards.

Ultimate Lithium Batteries (for your microphone) – $2 per battery
They're expensive, but they last. Sometimes all week.

500 GB LaCie Rugged Hard Drive – $75
So tough you can drop it from six feet. Get one with at least USB 3.0 so it works on your computer and will make your editor happy.

How to shoot an interview

Whether your movie features consumers, execs, or colleagues, interviews are the core of most business movies. They're more difficult to shoot than you'd think, so before you put yourself in the hot seat, practice interviewing someone who will cut you slack, like a colleague or a family member. That way, you can work out the kinks, get to know your equipment, and become comfortable in your new role.

Once you're ready, here are some basics to make yours look and sound good.

Find a quiet spot
I know it sounds weird, but good audio is even more important than a good picture. That's why I recommend the wireless lav microphone. Having the mic close to your interviewee gives you the same effect as talking to someone right in front of you. You can feel their voice as much as you can hear it. It's clear, it's rich, and it sounds right. On the other hand, when you use the mic built into the camera, even if it's only eight feet away, mics are like sound magnets, so it will also pick up every air conditioner, fan, and fridge in the neighborhood.

Once you find a quiet place, shut all the doors and turn off all cell phones. Now you're sounding good.

Within that quiet room, pick your spot
Where you place your interviewee is the key to getting good quality. Pick a space that's quiet and bright enough to see the color of your interviewee's eyes. And unless

it's important to your project, select a place where the background doesn't distract from your respondent.

<u>Find a window and place your interviewee next to it</u>
At first, film your interviews in the daytime. It's easier to make them look good in that environment; night filming often requires you to study up on lighting, requiring a lot of learning to get it right.

People tend to look best when the light comes from the side and slightly in front of them (up to a 45° angle). Placing them next to a window works beautifully. Make sure you see the color of your interviewees' eyes without having to zoom in. And if you can see a bit of shine in the iris, you're golden.

On the other extreme, make sure their cheeks are normal skin color and not a shocking white from the harsh sunlight. If they are, move them a few feet away from the window or close one of the drapes.

Here are some no-no's:

Do not place people with the window behind them. It will make them look darker because the camera will adjust for the bright light behind them and render your interviewee as a shadow. When you're more skilled, you can use backlight to make them look amazing, but that can only be achieved with a lot of experience.

Do not rely on ceiling lights. They cast the shadows that make people look older, and no one likes that.

OPTIMAL INTERVIEW SET-UP
(also works reversed, with window on the left)

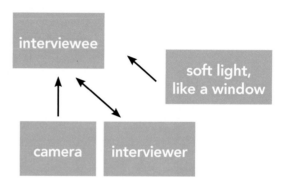

Do not light from the front (like a flash) It will give you clarity, but because the light is so harsh, your interview will look like an episode of *Cops*. Staring into the light will also make them squint and squirm, so it's even more like *Cops*.

Let's go back to what makes the interview look great. Check out the setup diagram to the left. That's an optimal interview setup without bringing in lights. It shows the best place for you and your interviewee to sit, and where to set up the camera.

<u>Setting up the camera</u>
As shown in the diagram, place the camera in front of the person you're interviewing, and place yourself between the camera and the window. This accomplishes a few things: more of the subject's face will be

lit by the window, including their eyes. And because they'll be talking to you, their eyes will look slightly off-camera. For a reason I can't explain, people look better and more credible that way—virtually every documentary setup has their subjects speaking while looking off camera. Politicians and newscasters can get away with looking directly at the camera, but everyone else tends to look creepy. (Insert creepy politician joke here.)

The same unflattering effect happens if you place your interviewee in the center of the camera's frame. Center framing will also make your interviewee look like they're posing for a mug shot. Framing their eyes about one-third of the way from the edge will make them look better (as if staring toward a larger open space), and also gives you room for a "nametag" (the subject's identifying title on the screen, or "lower third" in movie-speak). Check out the sample photos on the right.

A bit about backgrounds and framing
Most people put way too much unnecessary thought

into the background, as if it's the star of the shot. (As my grandmother used to say, "Let's get a picture of you two in front of the restaurant.") You want viewers to pay more attention to the person you're filming, so try to keep your background simple, like an Apple commercial.

Featuring the background, as in the wide shot below left, is effective when you want a visual shortcut to let people know what this person is all about, like filming a chef in a kitchen or a teacher in a classroom. But you don't need a ton of background, just enough to create that shortcut. If your camera is good enough, blur the background so you just get a hint of it, but keep the focus on your interviewee.

Framing close, like the sample shot below right, is effective for capturing emotion and making people believe. Just make sure you leave room for your interviewee to shift or sway, because they always do. And of course, leave room for their nametag, or the "lower third."

OPTIMAL INTERVIEW WIDE FRAMING

OPTIMAL INTERVIEW CLOSE-UP FRAMING

If you can afford it and have a skilled cameraperson, set up both shots so your editor can choose the one that best brings out the interviewee's quote.

It will take some practice, so try getting your colleagues to model for you first. They can use the opportunity to say something nice to their kid on camera, or you can try to get them to confess to something and cry like they're on *Oprah*.

How to shoot B-roll and action

The best shots always come from a good plan. All directors do it, even the bad ones, and it doesn't take much time to create a plan. Certainly less than all that futzing around when you're not prepared.

Developing a plan starts with visualizing your story, especially your opening and closing, then putting together a shot list. Do that and you'll be in command of your shoot, efficiently and systematically plowing through the filming.

When you're planning shots, you want to think of clear, literal ways to make your point. But also try to think of symbolic ways to show the subtext or implication of what you want to say. If you want to show someone struggling, film them walking up stairs or a hill. If you want to show their need for freedom, film them busting out of their front door. Showing things symbolically can often bring more meaning than the obvious images.

And never forget the magic of everyday shots, like people making orange juice, texting, or walking down the street. We can all relate to daydreaming during these mundane

actions because it comes across as if the person is thinking rather than speaking, and that can be powerful.

Here's a sample shot list I put together for a consumer insights project for a car company. It featured a real woman who chose family over a career. First we order the shots by theme so we can visualize it as we plot the story, then we reorder them by location and some other factors so everything can be shot efficiently. That's exactly how the movies do it. We also leave time for any off-the-cuff ideas that come up during the shoot. There's always magic in spontaneity.

SHOT LIST BY THEME:

Establishing Shots
- Neighborhood
- Home exterior
- Home interior
- Photos on walls
- Kids' rooms

Hero Shots
- Portrait far
- Portrait near
- Thinking
- Looking outside
- Portrait with car
- Holding something she feels represents her
- Something that represents her aspirations for her kids, like a diploma

Mom Shots
- Photos of kids when they were babies
- Mom in kitchen, with kids
- With kids in backyard
- With kids watching TV
- With kids in kids' bedroom
- Doing homework with kids
- Schoolwork on fridge
- With kids at park

Daily Life Shots
- Brands she likes
- Listening on phone
- Texting on phone
- On computer (hands as well)
- Where/how she relaxes
- Exercising
- Walking down her street
- Grocery list
- Making lunches
- Pouring coffee

Car Shots
- Grabbing keys, purse
- Walking toward car
- Everybody getting in
- Opening door
- Turning ignition
- Car interior
- Kid stuff in car
- Kids buckling up
- Driving car
- Kids in car while driving

- Trunk
- Her car approaching

NOW IN SHOOTING ORDER

Because we're filming real people, not actors, it's important to work with his/her mindset and possible sensitivities. I do the interview first so our hero loves us by the time we start invading her house and filming her kids. Here are the rest of the shots in the order of how we film them, both for her comfort and the efficiency of filming all your shots in a location while you're there. Movies also do this, which is why they always shoot their scenes in a completely different order than they appear in the film's narrative.

At/In Car
We do the car stuff first because she already knows that the project is for an auto company and expects it, plus it's a key requirement from our client.

- Grabbing keys, purse
- Walking toward car
- Everybody getting in
- Opening door
- Turning ignition
- Car interior
- Kid stuff in car
- Kids buckling up
- Driving car
- Kids in car while driving

At Park

We do the park next so everyone has fun—moms always take pride in watching their kids having a good time. If I get a cute shot, I'll show it to our mom hero so she loves us even more. Playing at the park also wears the kids out so they'll be more manageable when we get home. I do the car portrait there because there's often a lot of sun and our mom will be wearing sunglasses. It will make her look glamorous, and therefore, more heroic.

- Her car approaching
- Opening trunk and pulling out kids' stuff
- Playing with kids at park
- Portrait with car
- Loading up the car with kids

Back at House

When we get back to the house, we film the kid stuff first to get the most out of them while they're still sane.

- Kids in their bedrooms
- With kids in backyard
- With kids watching TV
- With kids in kitchen
- Doing homework with kids

When we're done with the kids, we do the walk outside the house so mom can have a moment of peace. While we're out there, we also grab the neighborhood shot. Then back into the house to finish up.

- Neighborhood (from her house)
- Walking down her street

We do the portraits next because mom is feeling loving and open. Also, we have many shots ahead and I want to catch her while she has still has energy.

- Holding something she feels represents her
- Something that represents her aspirations
- Something representing aspiration for kids, like a diploma
- Portrait far
- Portrait near
- Thinking
- Looking out

Finally, we take into account mom's energy level, and we do the simple action shots that are easy for her.

- On computer (hands as well)
- Where/how she relaxes
- Exercising
- Making lunches
- Pouring coffee
- Listening on phone
- Texting on phone

Once I finish the interviews, I'll do the portraits and action so we can clear out and let her get on with her day while our other cinematographer films the interior stuff.

- Home interior
- Photos on wall
- Grocery list

We shoot the home exterior when we're on our way out and heading back to the car.

In this case, the whole thing takes about an hour and a half, because we wanted to include the park. Otherwise, it should take about an hour.

You're probably thinking, "That's a lot of shots for a three-minute movie." And you're absolutely right. We film that many because we have to; it's our business. You probably won't have to shoot half as many unless you're doing a ten-minute movie. I just wanted you to see the thought process to inspire your own ideas.

The process of shooting and cutting yourself some slack
When I first started shooting movies, I put a lot of pressure on myself to get each shot right the first time. That was stupid. Even the most experienced cinematographers take three or four shots before they feel they have it right. And when they do, they still shoot one more for "insurance" or "safety" or "luck."

Take a cue from the professionals and give yourself the time and room to screw up. That keeps the stress at bay, produces better shots, and helps you get more efficient. And don't delete your shots while you're shooting. It takes too much time and makes you too self-critical. If you have doubts, just take another shot. You can always delete later, and sometimes what you think is a "bad" shot on location reveals itself to be usable when you're in the editing room.

Finally, shoot everything for at least five seconds, and if you're doing a camera move like a pan, hold for at least two seconds before your move, then at least two seconds after. This will make editing much, much easier. If you want to understand why, try editing a sequence. You'll quickly see that having the extra cushion of footage on either end of a shot is invaluable. And have some fun. It beats being in the office.

Editing on your own
I absolutely love editing, even more than shooting. It's like taking a Tasmanian devil and taming it into something affectionate and expressive. As I said earlier, I always start with the music. I find it easier to edit to a beat and I draw inspiration from the feeling the music generates, and it puts me in a better mood.

The software to start with is iMovie. Yes, the professionals will laugh at you, but forget them. iMovie will do 80% of what their software does and it's a million times easier to learn. Once you get the hang of it, it's amazing fun. And it's also super cheap—around $15, I think.

If you go with iMovie, you must make me a promise: pinky-swear not to use any of the gimmicky effects built into it. Please, please, please start with straight cuts. Your work will look more professional and cinematic. Most of iMovie's effects will only make you look like a clown.

Once you use iMovie for a few months, you might want to graduate to something with a bit more muscle. I suggest Final Cut. It's an easy transition from iMovie and it's a great program. If you have a Windows machine, Adobe

Premiere is also a fantastic program, but it's not as easy to learn as Final Cut, especially if you've used iMovie.

Stock footage

Stock footage sites like *pond5.com* or *bigstockphoto.com* have lots of footage you can get for $20 to $100. Big Stock Photo also has a subscription that's super cheap. Getty and Shutterstock have higher quality footage, but theirs usually starts at about $200 and they make you fill out a form on how you'll use it. So I'd start with the cheaper ones first.

Stock music

If your movie is confidential or only going to be seen by 20-or-so people, it might be fine to use unlicensed music (like your favorite songs in your iTunes library), but it's always a risk. It's much safer to use stock music. Stock music also comes in instrumental form which is actually much easier to work with when your movie has dialogue, like interviews or narration.

Stock music sites like *PremiumBeats.com* are pretty cheap and have tons of good music. *AudioNation.com* and *NewWestCollection.com* have even better music, but it costs about $150 a song. *AudioNation.com* has a nonprofit rate of something like $5, so I often try that first, then if I want it, I buy it at full price. Both sites give you a choice of short versions (usually one minute or under), and full-length versions (usually two to three minutes), and a set of loops, making it easier to cut the music to your required length. And buying stock material means it's legal to use anywhere you want, which will make your lawyers happy.

There is one challenging factor about finding the right stock music. It's hard to search for the right track because music is not visual and also so subjective—you end up testing a lot of samples. I usually search by the instrument I think I might like, then by the overall feeling I'm trying to convey. "Relaxing acoustic guitar," for example. It still takes up to an hour to find the perfect song, but it's worth it—there's no better way to make your movie sing than having really good music.

WEBSITES FOR STOCK MATERIAL

PHOTO & FOOTAGE SITES:
dreamstime.com
pond5.com
bigstockphoto.com
shutterstock.com
istockphoto.com
gettyimages.com

MUSIC SITES:
newwestcollection.com
premiumbeats.com
audionation.com
audiojungle.com

How To Get the Most Out of Professionals

When you have a high-stakes movie to make, I strongly advise hiring professionals. They will make your movie look and sound better, and you'll be freed up to do what you do best. (And seeing professionals in action is a great way to learn.)

Working with them can be squirrelly, though. Most need some handholding to understand what you're looking for, and if you need them to stay out of your way for something like a consumer insights interview, you have to tell them.

It's also key that you like them personally and feel like you want to hang out. You might spend ten hours a day together, or travel on the road with them for a week. That's a long time to be with someone who makes your ears hurt.

Here's how I would go about finding, selecting, and managing a professional.

Finding them

Finding professionals is as easy as running a Craigslist ad in the "movie crew" section of "gigs."

Here's what I would put in your ad:

- Description of the project (no need to put much, certainly not enough to compromise confidentiality)

- Dates you need them (if it's an editor, include a day or two of buffer, since timelines always shift)

- The kind of equipment they'll need (see "For videographers, insist on..." on the next page)

- Request for their day rate (they all charge by the day or half-day; never by the hour). A good videographer is $600-$1,500 per day; a good editor is $300-$1,000 per day

- A request for a link to their reel

You'll probably get 100 replies. Selecting the right one out of these 100 candidates isn't too tough. Here's how I cull it down to my top five. Did they…

- …supply everything you asked for in the ad and write a decent email? (that should cut it down to 50)

- …give you a rate that fits your budget? (down to 35)

- …have the equipment you need? (down to 25)

- …have a well-crafted reel that looks similar to what you envision? (down to ten)

- …ask at least some questions about what you need the movie to do? (Yay, down to five!)

After that, I suggest phone calls with your candidates to go over the project and ask how they'd approach it. Again, no need to compromise confidentiality; they care more about the shooting situation. If you have any special requirements, like needing them to stay in the background, ask them if they're okay with that. Don't wait until the shoot.

The professional that sounds confident (and someone you can spend a week with) is your winner.

What you should expect from a pro
You hired a pro to take your project up a notch or two, so they should have complete command of their craft, good equipment, and the ability to give you more in less time. They should also ask you intelligent questions to learn more about what you need.

For videographers, insist on:
- Wireless lavalier microphones (I use the Sennheisers I recommended earlier), also called lav, lapel, or clip mics.

- Cinematic camera with interchangeable lenses and XLR audio (I use a Canon C100 that has two XLRs and is compatible with any Canon lens). This will get you that creamy background blur. The XLRs will allow them to use high-end microphones like Sennheisers.

- If shooting executives or a high-end interview, ask for stay-cool, three-point, color-correct lighting with a softbox (I use Fiilex LEDs). Ask your videographer not to bring lights if you're shooting consumers. They can get overwhelmed, or worse, begin playing to the camera.

- And of course, they should show up on time and look like they know what they're doing.

Here's what you should do to get the best out of your videographer:

Give them a clear description of what you need and what the situation is. This is key for videographers because they need to know what kind of equipment to bring for the shoot. If you have an eight-person focus group, a good videographer should insist on bringing an additional videographer with a second camera. No single cameraperson can cover eight people, especially when it seems like the ones on the ends of the table are doing most of the talking. Even with a great videographer, you'll end up with so many camera swings, the footage will make you dizzy.

At the same time, listen to your videographer's recommendations on how to seat people so the camera can film everyone's face. A semicircle is a whole lot better than a conference table with people on both sides. I once tried to film a focus group around a conference table; it looked terrible, and I was worn out from moving back and forth between opposite sides of the room. Also, listen to what the videographer says about sound. In that same focus group, everyone came in with Doritos bags from the lobby and the client wouldn't let me take them away. The result: a swingy, nauseating video with a soundtrack of crinkling chip bags.

If it's a long day, feed your videographer. I once had a shoot at a market research facility with ten clients in the back room. I got two 15-minute breaks to eat, and when I came back for the first one, all the food was gone. The facility then ordered more food and agreed to keep it out of the client room, but guess who it was delivered to? Yup, those vultures ate my food again. For the rest of the day, all I could think about was how hungry I was. I got good footage, but I knew it would have been better if I'd concentrated solely on what they hired me for. So keep the crew in mind when it's lunchtime – a fed crew is a happy crew.

Finally, if your shoot is confidential, have your videographer sign an NDA (non-disclosure agreement) and tell him/her to give you the SD cards at the end of the day, rather than waiting for him/her to put them on a hard drive. That way, you know you've got every copy.

<u>What you should do to get the best from your editor</u>
Be clear: give the editor specific direction on both the information your movie is imparting and the mood you want to create. Again, if it's confidential, have him/her sign an NDA so you can get into details about your project, and you can also request they not work in a public place (these days, editors can work at the coffee shop). Lastly, emphasize the most important things you want your viewers to come away with:

- Your two or three key messages

- An emotional direction—something like "the people in the movie should be heroic, likable, and friendly."

Give your editor a schedule and ask if they can keep to it. It should have the date you'll give them footage, when you expect the rough cut, the timeline for sending corrections back and forth, and the final delivery date.

The rough cut is the editor's version of a rough draft, but it's done in person so the two of you can go over the movie, make changes, and try out ideas—on the fly. Chances are your editor will want you to go to their studio because most have computers and large screens too big to travel. It's tempting to ask your editor to just post it to you on Dropbox, but if you do that, you'll spend far more time going back and forth with downloads and corrections than the rough-cut session would take. All that back and forth can take weeks. By

going to the rough cut, you can be done in two hours and end up with a much better final movie.

When you're there, there will be some things in the rough cut that look unfinished or just plain wrong—the color of the shots, the crispness of the cuts, the ending of each piece of music, the level of the sound. Fear not, these are tasks editors typically do once the rough-cut session is over and corrections are made in the final cut.

That said, I like to buck tradition, so when our clients come to view a rough cut, I make sure it looks as close to perfect as possible. It's not only more fun that way, but I've found people can envision the final movie more easily, so I believe it's well worth the extra time.

That's it, compadres. If you have any questions, go to gettotheheartbook.com and click on "ask away."

REFERENCES

Chapter 1

Dr. Paul Zak, "Why Your Brain Loves Good Storytelling," *Harvard Business Review,* October 28, 2014.

The Wizard of Oz, directed by Victor Fleming, Metro-Goldwyn-Mayer, 1939.

Sudden Impact (Dirty Harry series), directed by Clint Eastwood, Warner Bros., 1983.

National Lampoon's Animal House, directed by John Landis, Universal Pictures,1978.

The Godfather, directed by Francis Ford Coppola, Alfran Productions / Paramount Pictures, 1972.

Star Wars, directed by George Lucas, Lucasfilm Ltd. / 20th Century Fox, 1977.

Christopher J. Frank, Paul Magnone, *Drinking from the Fire Hose: Making Smarter Decisions Without Drowning in Information* (New York: The Penguin Group, 2011) XXIV.

Chapter 2

Ira Glass, "Ira Glass on Storytelling Part 2: On Finding Great Stories," PRI Public Radio International, YouTube, uploaded on August 18, 2009, https://www.youtube.com/watch?v=KW6x7lOIsPE.

Chapter 3

Nancy Duarte, *Slide:ology: The Art and Science of Creating Great Presentations* (Sebastopol: O'Reilly Media, 2008) 64.

Chapter 4

Dr. Keith Oatley, "How Cues on the Screen Prompt Emotions in the Mind," in *Psychocinematics: Exploring Cognition at the Movies,* edited by Arthur P. Shimamura (Oxford; New York: Oxford University Press, 2013) 276.

M. Carolyn Clark, Marsha Rossiter, "Narrative Learning in Adulthood," *New Directions for Adult & Continuing Education* 119 (2008) 177.

Frank/Magnone, *Drinking from the Fire Hose,* XXIV.

Jonathan Haidt, *The Happiness Hypothesis: Finding Modern Truth in Ancient Wisdom* (New York: Basic Books, 2006) 3-5.

Birgit Wolz, "Cinema as Alchemy for Healing and Transformation," in *The Cinematic Mirror for Psychol-*

ogy and Life Coaching, edited by Mary Banks Gregerson (New York: Springer-Verlag, 2010) 207, 212.

Chapter 5
Dr. William Casebeer and Dr. Paul Zak, "Future of Storytelling Conference," May 16, 2013

Chapter 6
Dr. Paul J. Zak, "Why Inspiring Stories Make Us React: The Neuroscience of Narrative," *Cerebrum: the Dana Forum on Brain Science*, 2015:2, http://www.dana.org/Cerebrum/2015/Why_Inspiring_Stories_Make_Us_React__The_Neuroscience_of_Narrative/

John P. Kotter and Dan S. Cohen, "Gloves on the Boardroom Table: from Jon Stegner," in *The Heart of Change*, (Boston: Harvard Business Press, 2010) quoted in Chip and Dan Heath, *Switch: How to Change Things When Change is Hard* (New York: Broadway Books, 2010), 12-13.

Chapter 7
Waiting for Superman, directed by Davis Guggenheim, Paramount Vantage, 2010.

Frank/Magnone, *Drinking from the Fire Hose*; XXII.

Chapter 9
Dr. Carl Plantinga, "The Affective Power of Movies," in *Psychocinematics: Exploring Cognition at the Movies*, edited by Arthur P. Shimamura (Oxford; New York: Oxford University Press, 2013) 101, 107.

Duarte, *Slide:ology*, 64.

Chapter 11
Duarte, *Slide:ology*, 218.

You're serious? I'm all done?

You're not just messing with me?

Why do I not believe you?

– Ted Frank

53747061R00125

Made in the USA
San Bernardino, CA
27 September 2017